1959

Drag racing defined: two high-stepping coupes blast off the starting line in the 1950s in a quarter-mile celebration of acceleration. The cars and technology of the sport have changed dramatically over the decades, but the passion for performance has not.

**A** *full house*

witnessed the arrival of NHRA

drag racing at The Strip at Las Vegas

Motor Speedway, a jewel in the

collection of supertracks that host

championship events. Immense

grandstands crowned by penthouse

suites provide a colorful backdrop

for the world's fastest motorsport.

"The U.S. Nationals in Indianapolis features about 1,000 competition cars. That's why NHRA drag racing is the **fastest car show** on earth."

~Gary Darcy, NHRA Vice President, Marketing

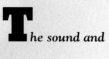

The sound and
fury of a Funny Car burnout
assaults the senses as driver
Scotty Cannon performs the
pre-race ritual of heating the
tires. Amidst trailing plumes of
vaporized rubber, Cannon grooms
the track surface to withstand
the instantaneous application of
over 6,000 horsepower.

The Fast Lane

The History of NHRA Drag Racing

50
1951 2001
YEARS OF POWER
NHRA
CHAMPIONSHIP DRAG RACING ™

Regan Books
An Imprint of HarperCollins*Publishers*

A TEHABI BOOK

Tehabi Books conceived, designed, and produced *The Fast Lane* and has developed and published many award-winning books that are recognized for their strong literary and visual content. Tehabi works with national and international publishers, corporations, institutions, and nonprofit groups to identify, develop, and implement comprehensive publishing programs. The name *Tehabi* is derived from a Hopi Indian legend and symbolizes the importance of teamwork. Tehabi Books is located in San Diego, California. www.tehabi.com

President: **Chris Capen**
Senior Vice President: **Tom Lewis**
Vice President, Development: **Andy Lewis**
Director, Sales & Marketing: **Tim Connolly**
Director, Corporate Publishing & Promotions: **Eric Pinkham**
Editorial Director, **Nancy Cash**
Art Director: **Curt Boyer**
Editor: **Terry Spohn**
Copyeditor: **Gail Fink**
Proofreader: **Lisa Wolff**
Indexer: **Ken DellaPenta**

Special thanks to the staff at the National Hot Rod Association for their contributions to the creation of *The Fast Lane*.

Acknowledgments and photography credits appear on page 204.

HarperCollins books may be purchased for educational, business, or sales promotional use. For information please write: Special Markets Department, HarperCollins Publishers Inc., 10 East 53rd Street, New York, NY 10022.

First Edition

Printed on acid-frree paper

Library of Congress Cataloging-in-Publication Data has been applied for.

ISBN 0-06-039405-6

Printed through Dai Nippon Printing Co., Ltd. in Hong Kong.

01 02 03 04 05 10 9 8 7 6 5 4 3 2 1

"Drag racing is **a sport** where there is **no limit.**"

—GARY SCELZI, NHRA TOP FUEL DRIVER

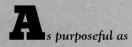

As purposeful as an arrow and as specialized as a scalpel, a Top Fuel dragster reduces drag racing to its most elemental forces: power, speed, and spectacle.

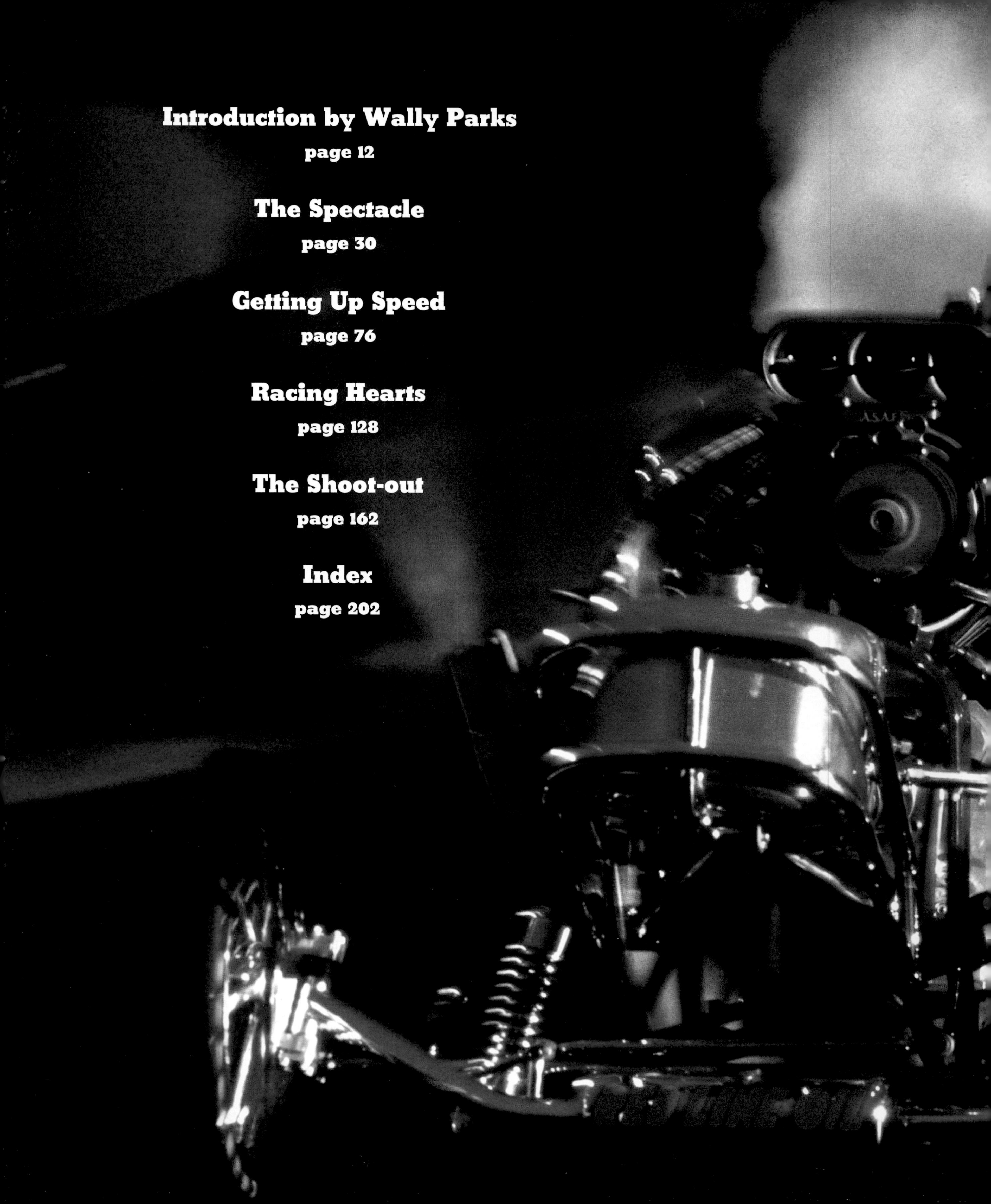

Stuff a high
and mighty supercharged hemi
engine into a short-wheelbase
Fuel Altered and you have a
recipe for Pure Hell on wheels.

Introduction

1956

It probably started on the main street of some unknown little town, when the owners of two "horseless carriages" lined up side by side to determine whose mount was the quicker. That such streets were often called "main drags" probably had nothing to do with the fact that the sport of automotive acceleration became known as "drag racing." But it satisfied an inherent urge for contesting one's wheel-driven accomplishments, to the end that today it has become the biggest, most innovative, and closely competitive field of motorsport in the world.

Organized drag racing's evolution traces back to early speed trials conducted on dry lake beds in the California desert. They included timed qualifying runs for entry in racing classes ranging from sixty miles per hour to one hundred mph and over. Cars were lined up abreast, with rolling starts signaled from a pace car running alongside.

The earliest such events were randomly formed, with little control or organization and lots of natural safety hazards. A 1930s growth in dry lakes popularity prompted the formation of car clubs that bonded together as timing associations and soon developed new rules, classes, and procedures to help ensure safer conduct and the continuity of their desert events. World War II curtailed dry lakes racing, as the timing associations were voluntarily disbanded for the duration.

By 1945 a prewar trend had resurfaced and "hot rods," as they were now known, had fast become a national postwar phenomenon. Clubs and timing associations were reorganized and desert time trials were renewed, as hot rodders' activity picked up where it had left off.

But available lake beds were diminishing as surfaces deteriorated. Racing events were fewer and sometimes less safe. And there was a new need, among growing legions of car builders, for an alternative outlet for speed and performance contesting. Street racing, both risky and illegal, had become a problem in many communities far and wide—adding to already existing controversies and public disfavor for anything associated with the hot rod label.

This very clean Fiat-bodied A/Altered Mighty Mouse was the handiwork of Jack Doyle and Sonny Mazza, members of the Hi-Winders Club of Lynn, Massachusetts. Powered by a GMC-blown Chrysler hemi, it set a national speed record in 1959.

As interest increased and access to suitable dry lakes declined, the search began for a workable substitute. Shorter-course racing was a natural prospect, and various groups experimented with half-mile and quarter-mile acceleration distances, running cars singly or in pairs.

By 1951 the National Hot Rod Association had been formed, with *Hot Rod* magazine as its conduit to a fast-growing readership. The primary founders of NHRA were veteran dry lakes and salt flats racers. Each had served elected offices in the Southern California Timing Association (SCTA) and all were active in the generation of a new sport called drag racing.

NHRA was initially established as a car clubs umbrella organization. Its first objective was to promote safety in special activities for its members. Early on, it was evident there was a "need for speed" that had not been included as part of the curriculum for organized car club events. To fulfill this basic function, NHRA embarked on a full-scale program aimed at cultivating a promising new sport that might be accessible to any region.

Rules, standards, and operating procedures were "borrowed" from closely related experience gained at the dry lakes. Insurance, classes, and racing guidelines came later. Utilizing its established good relations with law enforcement and civic leaders, NHRA relied upon its affiliate clubs for support in attaining first-time drag racing facilities in many communities.

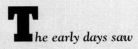

The early days saw organized drag racing spread quickly as NHRA ran its first major sanctioned event at Pomona, California in 1953.

News about the new sport of drag racing spread quickly through the underground network of car clubs. Members, above, wore their jackets as badges of honor when they gathered in garages and shops to talk about fast cars and good times. When a hot rodder needed a hand, there was seldom a lack of volunteers—and they were accomplished mechanics. The group at right managed this complete engine change at the drag strip in less than an hour.

By the mid-1950s NHRA had formed its "Drag Safari," later renamed "Safety Safari"—a team of experienced hot rodders led by an energetic California police officer. In its three years of coast-to-coast crusades, the Safari both introduced and educated its car club hosts, civic leaders, law enforcement officials, contestants, media, and the general public on the benefits and potentials of properly run "organized drag racing."

In the Safari's second year it became clear that a level of racing competition higher than the tour's Regional events was needed to satisfy the growing interest of member drag racers across the country. A solution to that prospect was NHRA's introduction of drag racing's first National Championships, contested in 1955 on an airbase runway near the exact geographical center of the United States, at Great Bend, Kansas. Its outcome led to following years of the "Nationals" in Missouri, Oklahoma, Michigan, and ultimately to the event's present home in Indiana, in 1961.

In keeping with its own growth and drag racing's popularity, NHRA had established a communications system that linked members and clubs with its operations center. Area Advisors, then Regional Advisors, were the first appointed—all volunteers. Their combined efforts laid the groundwork for what would become a progressive campaign for public appreciation.

By the end of the 1950s, NHRA had formed a Divisional system in seven geographic sections of the United States and Canada, led by seven full-time Division Directors. Carefully selected, and most often with wives in active support roles, they were the coordinators and overseers of NHRA's major functions in their individual territories and its personal tie with membership.

In pioneer years of drag racing, it was Division Directors and their Division Technical Directors who provided the bulk of input for compelling and constant refinement of competition rules. Their liaison with racers and track operators in their areas contributed priceless hands-on experience. Supported by their individual "Certification teams," DDs often performed miracles in event productions at makeshift facilities in the sport's infancy.

Ensuing years in drag racing's growth have added new challenges to what was once a basic mandate: providing and protecting a source for the safer enjoyment of creativity, speed, and performance on wheels. More than 140 member tracks are operated regularly under NHRA's sanction banner, accounting for over five thousand drag racing dates per year.

Vehicles, contestants, racetracks, fans, and supporters have been under the microscope of surveillance since the sport's maverick days fifty years ago. But NHRA's early slogans, "Dedicated to Safety" and "Ingenuity in Action," are still very much intact—remaining its paramount objectives.

Wally Parks

1964

This flying flagman at Houston Drag Raceway sends a small-block Chevy slingshot on its way.

Hot Rodding

Illegal street racing had been around as long as the automobile, but it took off after World War II, when GIs with enhanced mechanical skills and a love of speed and danger returned to civilian life. Stripped-down hot rods roamed the streets and often seemed menacing even when just prowling. But it was the sometimes-tragic crashes during illegal races that increasingly commanded headlines. While the "hot rod menace" was no doubt a bit overblown, racing on the increasingly crowded streets of postwar America had become a problem of major proportions-by 1950 and officials threatened a ban on hot rods.

But others favored a more constructive and probably more attainable approach to the problem—giving the kids a place to race safely. Soon the newly formed National Hot Rod Association would make this a keystone of its official policy.

1973

Hot rodding was a cultural phenomenon in the 1950s, and modern drag racing still pays homage to its hot rodding roots with race cars that evolved from the stripped-down Model Ts and '32 Ford roadsters of bygone days, bottom.

The NHRA Museum

The sport of drag racing has many meccas, from the ultra-modern drag strips at Chicago, Pomona, and elsewhere around the country to dozens of smaller strips where the action is hot and heavy with NHRA-sanctioned regional events every weekend. But like other major sports, it also has a hallowed hall where the main action is memory. It's the NHRA Motorsports Museum in Pomona, California, on the site of the first major NHRA-sanctioned event.

Opened in 1998, the museum hosts hot rod events, education classes, and an impressive display of drag racing's classic cars. A tour of the main exhibit room is a trip into the past and back again, a testament to the audacity and creativity of the early drivers and the technological advances in speed, safety, and beauty of the cars.

There's eye candy for every car lover, from a re-creation of Dick Kraft's Bug to John Force's 1989 Cutlass Funny Car to famous exhibition cars like Hemi Under Glass and Tommy Ivo's four-engine Showboat. Visitors find dragsters, stockers, Funny Cars, and Fuel Altereds from every era of the past fifty years. And they find memories.

You can almost hear the weekly radio promos for drag racing on "Sunday, Sunday, Sunday . . ."

But the museum is more than just a history lesson. It's a regular hangout for modern-day hot rod-ders who take part in events like the "Twilight Cruises" almost every Wednesday evening from March through November, a hot rod prom-enade that grew from one hundred to five hundred cars in its first year.

The NHRA Motorsports Museum's main exhibit room has a circumference of exactly a quarter mile and is home to some of the most famous race cars on the planet.

Bonneville

The Bonneville Salt Flats, a stretch of salt deposit left by the recession of an ancient lake, covers an area of approximately 160 square miles near what is now Interstate 80 in Utah. For decades before the hot rod era, Bonneville's glorious expanse of snow-white salt had been the site of various assaults on the land speed record—typically pursued by wealthy Englishmen. The salt flats, first tested as a racetrack in 1912, had become a mecca for racers because of its long, hard, smooth surface. In the years between the World Wars it had hosted a variety of increasingly streamlined vehicles in search of automotive glory.

Hot rodders began getting their turn in 1949, just before the debut of commercial drag races, when the Southern California Timing Association staged the first annual Bonneville National Speed Trials. At Bonneville, the fastest cars were geared so high that they accelerated slowly away from the starting line, usually needing an assist from another vehicle, and did not really get moving until almost out of sight.

This was quite unlike drag races, where cars charged off with tires smoking and engines screaming, and everything was over within a few ticks of the clock. Bonneville was about top speed, and cars made their runs individually. Drag racing was about acceleration from a standing start, and cars raced side by side. Still, many of the first standout drag racers, such as Art Chrisman and Mickey Thompson, honed their mechanical skills to a keen edge on the salt.

1949

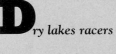

Dry lakes racers like these were at the heart of speed trial racing. From early cars like the Suite 16 Belly Tank racer and Sweet Sue, facing page, at El Mirage two generations ago, to the Indiana roadster at left who's a long way from home or the Competition Coupe, above, at Bonneville in 1991, the hot rod tradition has flourished in the desert.

WALLY PARKS

Wally Parks did not invent drag racing; history does not record the first side-by-side acceleration contest between cars. But NHRA, the organization Parks founded in 1951, gave the sport its form and structure and, most important, consistent leadership for fifty years.

Parks has the attributes of a leader: charisma, vision, and the ability to inspire others to work toward ambitious goals. He commands respect, but is quick to turn the spotlight onto the contributions of many others to the sport. Foremost among them is his wife, Barbara, steadfast in her support since the days when she typed membership cards and maintained NHRA's correspondence at the kitchen table.

Born in Oklahoma in 1913 and raised in Kansas, Parks found himself in the hotbed of hot rodding when his family moved to southern California. Two stripped-down Model Ts built as class projects in high school auto shop sparked his interest in cars. He built his own hot rod and became a regular in the thriving car club and clandestine street racing scenes.

Parks could write as well, and soon became the chronicler of the Southern California Timing Association (SCTA) in the '30s and '40s, reporting the exploits of racers on the dry lakes of southern California. When he became the first editor of *Hot Rod* magazine, he used its pages to preach the gospel of speed with safety.

His first encounter with organized drag racing was at a navy blimp base in Tustin, California, in 1950. The SCTA staged trials pitting motorcycles against cars. The final round came down to a roadster-versus-bike race. The car won, and Parks

was hooked. "I was impressed with drag racing from its very start," he said, "with its challenges of pitting brute horsepower against traction."

Overcoming hot rodding's "outlaw" image was a top priority for NHRA. "Street racing had become a major problem," Parks admitted. NHRA reached a milestone on the road to respectability with the success of the inaugural U.S. Nationals in Great Bend, Kansas, in 1955. It was NHRA's first chance to show its stuff. In the 1960s, ABC's *Wide World of Sports* coverage helped introduce NHRA drag racing to the rest of America.

As NHRA prospered, Parks steered it through the sometimes conflicting interests of professional entertainment and amateur competition. He has seen the sport grow from dusty airfields to spectacular stadium-style arenas.

Parks was the first recipient of *Car Craft* magazine's Ollie Award in 1969. He was *Popular Hot Rodding* magazine's Man of the Decade in 1972 and the Specialty Equipment Market Association's Man of the Year in 1973. He was drag racing's first inductee into the International Motorsports Hall of Fame in 1992, and in 1993 was inducted into the Motorsports Hall of Fame. He was named to the International Drag Racing Hall of Fame in 1994, and has been a director of the Automobile Competition Committee for the United States (ACCUS) since 1965.

Parks was president of NHRA through 1983, and chairman of the board through 1999. At eighty-three, he drove a recreation of his record-setting 1957 Plymouth Hot Rod Magazine Special on the Bonneville salt flats and the dry lakes of southern California.

Looking back at fifty years of history, Parks marvels at drag racing's growth. "NHRA's first-year enrollment reached more than five thousand. That the new association might ever reach today's mark of over eighty-five thousand never entered our minds—and that it might someday become the world's largest motorsports sanctioning body would have been unthinkable." For Wally Parks, the organization he founded, and legions of drag racers, achieving the unthinkable became routine.

**NHRA
25**

Wally Parks could turn a wrench and drive a race car as well as anyone—but it was his penchant for safety and his vision of drag racing's future that inspired the creation of NHRA.

NHRA Division Directors: Quarter-Mile Missionaries

They were disciples of drag racing, whose mission it was to spread the word, and they crossed the continent preaching the gospel of safety and speed. The early Division Directors were the founding fathers of the sport. They came from diverse backgrounds and regions, but shared a common vision.

"NHRA's original Division Directors were racers, car club members, area organizers, and genuine hot rod enthusiasts," recalled founder Wally Parks. "As NHRA's official spokesmen, Division Directors provided both leadership and guidance in their areas. In drag racing, theirs was 'the word.'"

The spark first struck on abandoned airfields in southern California had ignited a firestorm of interest. Converts clamored for information: What was drag racing? What were the rules? Who was in charge? NHRA created the field divisions to provide answers, partitioning the United States into seven

divisions. In those days, the presence of a representative was essential to the growth of NHRA, and the Division Directors became the consuls for championship drag racing.

The first four Division Directors were named in 1958: Ed Eaton (Northeast), Ernie Schorb (Southeast), Dale Ham (South Central), and Bob Daniels (North Central). Darrell Zimmerman (West Central), Jack Merrill (Northwest), and Bernie Partridge (Southwest) soon joined the fold. The foundation for a truly national organization was in place.

Personnel changes were few in those formative years. Lou Bond and Darwin Doll succeeded Ed Eaton, and Buster Couch eventually took the reins from Ernie Schorb. Most of them channeled their passion for racing into a lifetime profession. Darrell Zimmerman served as Division 5 Director for thirty-four years, then returned to the sport after a brief retirement. Daniels

became the general manager of Indianapolis Raceway Park, NHRA's flagship facility, and Partridge became NHRA's vice president of field operations.

The original Division Directors sacrificed jobs, comfort, and security for the fledgling organization. Partridge gave up his civil service job and took a $25 per-month pay cut—big money in those days—to become an NHRA staff member. Zimmerman left a lucrative job at an automobile dealership and never looked back.

The early directors brought missionary zeal to the sport. "I had been writing letters on behalf of our car club to Wally Parks when he became editor of *Hot Rod* magazine," remembered Dale Ham, NHRA's man in Texas. "I thought he had one hell of a dream for us all, and I just wanted to meet the guy."

For the early Division Directors, life was a blur of meetings, conferences, car shows, races, and roadside motels. They drove eighty thousand miles a year in Plymouth station wagons to meet with anyone who could have an impact on the sport.

"Those who weren't around then might think it was easy running no more than four national events a year during the '60s," noted Bob Daniels. "But they don't take into account all of the field work involved in establishing new tracks and working with public officials who still needed to be convinced of the importance of keeping kids off the streets with organized events."

"I had enough chicken dinners at the Kiwanis and Lions clubs to sink the *Queen Mary*," recalled Ham. "It was a hard sell initially, but when the 'big three' automobile manufacturers got involved, it gave us a lot more credibility."

The men were not alone in their remote outposts. Wives and children were members of the NHRA team, performing essential duties.

They sold tickets, gave out time slips, filed entries, and stuffed envelopes.

"We built fences and installed outhouses," said Bernie Partridge of his days in the Dust Devils car club. "P. J. [his wife Phyllis] worked the ticket sales, and after we got our first timing clocks, she was the first track recorder. P. J. worked in a tower built out of two-by-fours where she would list the cars' best runs on a blackboard."

They were in unknown territory. No policy manual told Darwin Doll how to deal with a chinchilla farmer who claimed the noise of open exhausts disturbed his animals. A judge sided with the farmer, so Darwin and the Sportsters Roadsters Association had to find a new site.

Despite the steep learning curve, these missionaries on wheels oversaw construction of dozens of drag strips, improved community relations, and brought order to the conflicting rules and procedures. The framework they built now supports 142 member tracks that conduct five thousand events and 1.5 million side-by-side races annually.

NHRA
27

Early Division Directors and NHRA officials, left, laid the foundation. NHRA's board of directors, right (left to right), Tom Compton, Wally Parks, Dallas Gardner, and Dick Wells, continues that stewardship of the sport.

The Safety Safari

NHRA initially focused its efforts on car shows and reliability runs, but by 1953 it was producing drag racing events. The first of these took place in April at the Los Angeles County Fairgrounds in Pomona, which is still the site of two premier NHRA events, the Winternationals and the NHRA Finals. Inspired by what they read about such events in *Hot Rod*, young automobile enthusiasts began forming car clubs from coast to coast and looking for places to hold legal drag races. There were small airports and decommissioned military airfields all over the country, but gaining access was contingent on posting liability insurance, which was of course contingent on the enforcement of

safety rules. Out of this need was born NHRA's Safety Safari.

On June 10, 1954, five young men struck out for the East to show how to set up races and keep them safe and to let the organizers in on a first-class insurance program. Heading the original Drag Safari, as it was then known, was Bud Coons, a former police sergeant who had been instrumental in establishing the drag strip at Pomona. Also along was Chic Cannon, who had considerable experience working with teenagers and young adults; Eric Rickman, *Hot Rod's*

ace photographer, who went along to document the events; Jim Nelson, one of the sport's early tech inspectors; and Bud Evans, who served as an announcer during the Safari tour. Twice more, such Safaris would tour the country. Together these trips put NHRA on the map to stay.

By the time the Safari finished its third trek in 1956, NHRA had helped organize regional competitions in at least twenty-five states. Within a decade, NHRA had sanctioned ten thousand events.

The Safety Safari has grown from its modest beginning, top. Today, crews prepare and repair racing surfaces to assure safety, and also operate the fast-acting rescue squads stationed at both ends of the track in case of a mishap.

Because Great Bend had limited overnight accommodations, NHRA moved its Nationals to Kansas City in 1956. The location and plant were more satisfactory, but the timing tower (inset) was still a far cry from those familiar to present-day fans.

The Spectacle

The shimmer and the haze, the colors and the music—if one thing has remained constant throughout the phenomenal growth and technological development that NHRA drag racing has experienced in the last fifty years, it's the explosion of color and sound at the drag strip. The cars are blurs of color, and the faster the car, the louder the sound and the more intense the pressure waves. To many, it's all about the part of the spectacle that can only be felt and heard. Nothing compares to the force field around a 6,000-horsepower machine. The flood of sensations from these hopped-up engines attacks your eardrums, pounds your chest, and makes your eyes water. And it is exactly this kind of bombardment that pulls both racers and their fans into drag racing like fans to a rock concert.

Now, opposite, and then (above)

But we've gotten ahead of ourselves here. We've peeked at the moment of meltdown, which is to give short shrift to how dynamic a day at the drags really is. In fact, drag racing is the most multifaceted sport there is, and the spectacle offers more than a fan can absorb in just one day. The best way to preview the variety of sensory delights is to come in right at the beginning of the action on a Saturday morning.

Competition begins early, with the arrival of the most ardent and dedicated bleacher bums, bleary-eyed and waiting for the coffee they consumed moments earlier to kick in. The first cars down the drag strip are known generically as "stockers," but more specifically they're in the Stock Eliminator or Super Stock Eliminator categories. Known as "Grocery Getters" in drag strip slang, these vehicles are hot-rod coupes, sedans, station wagons, and more. These street machines are not nearly as radical as the more exotic classes that will blast down the strip later in the day. Because a stocker is nearly identical to a car driven on the street by an average American, a car like this is known as the People's Eliminator, and their engines echo in the public address system.

"It's all about **fast cars** and friendly **people.**"

—MIKE TRINIDADE, NHRA FAN, MARYSVILLE, CALIFORNIA

Though the nitro-burning Top Fuelers and Funny Cars, bottom, are the stars of the show, true aficionados also appreciate the awesome variety of Sportsman race cars, top. Drag racing is truly a sport for every car buff.

Coming at you are a couple of good old-fashioned muscle cars, the Super Stock/G Automatic '72 Plymouth Challenger of Buzz Marconi, towerside, and the '68 Camaro SS/A of Tino Marquez in the Winston Lane. Marconi leaves expertly on his handicap start. Marquez is off the pad and on the rear bumper, a wheels-up start as the driver from Riverside begins banging through the gears in hot pursuit. Oohhh, the Plymouth is making tracks and it won't be caught as Marconi turns an elapsed time of 9.88 seconds.

Seasoned railbirds know to tune their AM radios to the extreme left-hand side of the frequency band for the public address system simulcast of a micro-transmitter whose range is just a mile or two beyond the periphery of the grounds. Over the open microphone in the timing tower, you can hear partially open throttles and tires spinning in a patch of water as the competitors warm them in anticipation of maximum traction. A second and a half later the same sound waves reach the race fans in the parking lot.

hat sets NHRA drag racing apart from all

other sports is the close and casual contact fans can have with their idols. Here, Funny Car champion

John Force greets some of the faithful near the end of a long day.

itromethane fumes can make even strong men weep. The members of the Bill Miller Engineering Top Fuel team don gas masks as they warm up the engine before a run.

For some fans, the starting line at Route 66 Raceway near Chicago,

Illinois, is the only place to sit. For others, it's halfway down the track, where they can glimpse a driver's battle to keep a drifting fueler in

the groove or off the wall, or perhaps see the shoe of a late but quicker machine reel in an opponent.

With flames erupting from her engine's exhaust pipes, teenage Top Fuel driver Cristen Powell, top, manhandles her tire-smoking machine. When the twin parachutes blossom at the end of a run, Top Fuel drivers decelerate at five times the force of gravity.

Towerside is the Super Comp dragster of Ed Davenport, and although he is competing in Super Comp, to call him a Sportsman racer is not entirely accurate, as this is a guy who races professionally year round in his big-block Chevy-powered dragster. Davenport is facing local hitter Steve Green and his Clean and Green center-steer '23 T roadster, blown with a Roots-type Mooneyham 6-71 huffer and injected on gasoline.

The patter of the PA announcers continues. The radio broadcast soothes the nerves of early arrivals who wait not so patiently to wind their way into the parking lot and the sea of cars that has begun to envelop the grounds alongside the shutdown area of the drag strip.

"When I was young I wanted to put on a firesuit and blast through the traps at over 200 mph."
—WILLIAM P. CARRELL, NHRA FAN, HOUSTON, TEXAS

Davenport has him out of the hole and both cars grunt at the 330-foot mark . . . okay, they are side by side at half track as the throttle stops disengage and it looks like Steve Green just might put the most fabled racer of this class on the trailer. Attention in the pits. We need Federal-Mogul dragster to the lanes, please. First call for Federal-Mogul dragster…

As fans make their way into parking spaces, they might catch sight of the Super Comp racers with parachutes in full blossom, the laundry dancing in the wind as the cars slow enough for their carbon brakes to restrict the rotation of the big slicks. The Sportsman crowd is just getting their ya-yas out, testing their mettle as mechanics and drivers, oblivious to the fact that each run down the strip helps prepare the surface for the conquering lions of NHRA drag racing, the Top Fuelers, the Funny Cars, and the Pro Stockers. The gasoline-burning Sportsman machines continue to lay down rubber on what is developing into a "groove," other-wise known as a layered contact patch of quite thoroughly compressed stickum on a racing surface that was "green" not long ago.

Meanwhile, fans make their way through the turnstiles to soak up the ambience of the manufacturers' midway, the food vendors, and the T-shirt trailers. It is a kaleidoscope of color and smells, with the scents of grilled meat and popcorn competing with the warm, pungent odor of various fuels drifting out of the pits as competitors warm up and leak test their engines. The morning session of stockers and Super Classes has given way to Competition Eliminator, a wide variety of exotic gas-burning machines equalized by a system of handicapped starts. These are dragsters, roadsters, and doorslammers propelled by flatheads, six bangers, and V-8s made by anybody from American Motors to Chrysler.

Next up, Frank Aragona Jr., the record holder in G/Econo Dragster, who will spot the K/Altered '40 Ford of Allyn Armstrong six tenths of a second. Oh! A red-light start by Armstong nullifies his advantage and the win is Aragona's before he even turns a tire.

The pits are one of the most popular places at the drag strip. Here fans can not only get autographs from their favorite drivers, but also see the cars up close and watch as busy crews prepare them for the next race.

Only in this sport can fans converge on the pits and gather next to race teams as they prepare their machines for competition.

Pro Stock Truck to the lanes, please. Pro Stock Truck, this is your first call to the staging lanes . . .

Ground zero shifts every time somebody new spins the aircraft starter on the blower snout of a nitro-powered race car, a whining noise that alerts the nitromaniacs that more controlled detonations are imminent. It is an hour before the dragsters and the Funny Cars will follow the starter's order and launch off the pad, and the idea is to create some heat in the engine. The air is filled with racket as crew members from various teams light off Top Fuel dragsters at will. Fanatics converge on a given fuel as the overdriven fuel system spews raw nitromethane out of its exhaust and the car idles and lurches on jack stands. By now, some fans have left the pit areas and their madding sea of machinery and humanity and have grabbed seats to watch the Federal-Mogul qualifying races, a slightly tamer version of the nitro-burning headliners. These same motorheads will also watch the Pro Stockers grind through the gears in their gas-powered coupes, trucks, and motorcycles. But the rest crave the bang of nitro cars, the machines that burn the most exotic hydrocarbon on the premises. These fans hang out in the pits until the last fuel car has made its way to the staging lanes. Then and only then do they scramble for the grandstands like tardy air travelers boarding a plane that is about to begin backing away from the terminal.

Racers use an endearing set of euphemisms for a blown engine— "tossing" a rod, "lifting" a blower—but when it happens, what they really mean is mayhem.

he two-wheeled warriors of Pro Stock Bike are

the only participants in drag racing to attack the quarter mile without a roll cage or safety harness,

choosing instead to exceed 190 mph with nothing more than leathers and a helmet between them-

selves and the asphalt.

On the Line

The starting procedure did not get formalized for a number of years. In the beginning there was just someone with a flag, or sometimes a flashlight (recall the predawn race in *American Graffiti*). Flaggers did their job with skill and often with considerable courage, but there could be a lot of disagreement about when the go signal was actually given, and false starts were common. More sophisticated devices, such as a foul button, were developed over time. The starter kept the tip of the flag on the foul button, and if a driver left before it was yanked skyward the starter triggered a red light, which meant automatic disqualification. Eventually the now-universal Christmas Tree was developed and first appeared at national events in 1964.

With the Nomex-suited drivers, *left*, contemplating the task ahead, crew members pull belts taut, snap buckles, and hook up restraints while others take a final look at fittings and connections that were unconnected back in the pits only a few minutes before. Then, fired up, it's time to ease up to the starting beam, *bottom*. The Christmas Tree, *top*, will trigger the start of the race.

Don Garlits once dubbed a fueler a "parts-eating monster." Mishaps like the engine explosion that blew the body off this fuel Funny Car are rare now, and safety precautions protect drivers and onlookers.

"In the car, no matter what the **explosion,** I know exactly what to do: brake handle, parachute, oxygen. But if I'm outside and I hear a car blow up, **I duck.**"

—JOHN FORCE, NHRA DRIVER

THE BEAN BANDITS

Pappy Hart's track Santa Ana gets honors as the first drag strip, but it was at another strip near San Diego where the first drag racers emerged as folk heroes. It was called Paradise Mesa and the racers were called the Bean Bandits. Fierce competitors and shrewd showmen as well—they dressed in straw hats and cotton whites and were always quotable— the Bandits were forerunners of drivers like Tommy Ivo, Jungle Jim Liberman, and John Force. Though truly a rainbow coalition, with blacks, whites, and Asians as well as Hispanics, they were commonly called "beaners," and they took this derogatory expression and turned it around. "We'll show them," said Carlos Ramirez. "We'll leave our name on the tips of their tongues."

Ramirez sometimes drove for the Bandits, but more often it was Joaquin Arnett, their head honcho

1953

"We'll leave our name on the tips of their tongues."
— CARLOS RAMIREZ, BEAN BANDIT

and chief innovator. Arnett was a master at extracting maximum horsepower from a flathead Ford at minimum cost, and he was also one of the first racers to penetrate the secrets of nitro. In a day when dragsters were ordinarily assembled from junkyard parts, Arnett built from scratch, welding chassis together from steel tubing and hand-forming the bodywork. There was a whole series of Bean Bandits dragsters, both front engine and mid-engine, which set and reset speed and elapsed-time records in the '50s. Arnett won the NHRA's first Southern California Championships at Pomona, and the Bandits toured the country and got appearance money when that sort of thing was almost unheard of.

In the late 1950s they retired to raise their families but thirty years later they were back, at El Mirage and Bonneville, with Arnett still as sharp as ever at extracting maximum performance from limited finances. In 1992, when he was inducted into the International Drag Racing Hall of Fame in Florida, he and his compadres drove three thousand miles cross-country, accepted honors with singular wit and grace, then drove back home.

The Bean Bandits dragster, top, can be seen today in the NHRA Motorsports Museum. Joaquin Arnett built the car from scratch, rather than adapting an existing car's frame as other racers did.

Art Chrisman's Time Machine

No. 25 is in its eighth decade as a race car. It started out in the 1930s as a dry lakes "Modified"—one of its drivers was Wally Parks—then was turned into a drag racing machine in 1950 by Art Chrisman. But not just any drag racing machine. It was the first to top 140 mph, in February 1953. Three months later, it was on the cover of *Hot Rod* along with the words "The West's Most Fabulous Dragster." This was the first use of the term "dragster," and it has stuck ever since. With Chrysler power replacing the flathead Ford, No. 25 raced down

the sands of Daytona Beach. And it made the first pass at NHRA's first National Championship event, in Great Bend, Kansas. The photo at right shows it at Perryville Air Strip, near Phoenix, where final eliminations were run after a rainout in Kansas.

No. 25 was soon rendered obsolete by the advent of slingshots, but it lives on into the twenty-first century, lovingly restored by Chrisman when the nostalgia bug first bit in the late 1970s. That's Art in the photo (standing), with his brother Lloyd, who has since passed on, as has Art's nephew (and fellow Hall of Famer) Jack Chrisman.

But Art still thrives as a builder of premier

1955

street rods, and he can also be seen at the drags helping his son Mike tune his state-of-the-art Nostalgia Junior Fueler.

In top-flight NHRA competition, another of Art's nephews, Jerry Toliver, is a fast-rising fuel Funny Car pilot. There may be no other drag racing family so illustrious, and probably no one machine so wonderfully evocative of drag racing's beginnings as No. 25, in which Chrisman made his first pass at Santa Ana a couple of months before Jerry Toliver was born.

1961

Jack Chrisman sits in the cockpit of the Howard Cam Twin Bear in
the Pomona pits during the 1961 Winternationals. In those days, horsepower came first, and aerodynamic styling was an afterthought.

How Many Engines is Enough?

Even before the term "dragster" was coined, racers were thinking about different places to put the engine. At first it was always in front of the cockpit, as with any hot rod, but soon enough some innovators were putting it behind. This put more weight on the rear tires, but often at the expense of directional stability: With limited means of lining up their sights, most drivers simply couldn't tell when they were getting crossed up. Even though there were exceptions such as Lyle Fisher and Red Greth's Speed Sport, machines configured this way quickly got a reputation for spooky handling.

Racers always believed that if too much was just enough, more was even better. And so it was inevitable that they would see what could be done with twin engines. The Bean Bandits were again pace-setters, as was Mickey Thompson. In the late 1950s there was a rush of enthusiasm for twins, with the Howard Cam Bear and John Peters and Nye Frank's Freight Train being the most successful of a large contingent. Lefty Mudersbach tried three engines, and Tommy Ivo ordered a four-engine car from Kent Fuller, who was just beginning his reign as the premier dragster designer of his time.

Some twins had the engines side-by-side, and others had them in tandem. But Lloyd Scott's Bustle Bomb was unique: It had one engine (a Cadillac) behind the rear axle and the other (an Oldsmobile) in front of the driver. At NHRA's first National Championships the Bustle Bomb became the first dragster to top 150 mph.

The early experiments included one other novel configuration, "sidewinders," with the engine mounted transversely and chain driven. Although one such machine, built by Creighton Hunter (one of C. J. Hart's partners at Santa Ana),

1961

1963

In the heyday of the Top Gas Eliminator class, twin-engined dragsters dominated the division. The "Freight Train," above, was among the most famous of the breed. With the demise of Top Gas, the multi-engined behemoths joined the dinosaurs in extinction. Tommy Ivo's "Showboat," facing page, not only featured four engines, but four-wheel drive, as well.

A *very young Eddie Hill works on his twin Pontiac at the 1961*

Nationals under conditions modern drag racers would consider primitive.

had the engine in front of the driver, usually it was behind. The concept had definite advantages, but there always was the problem of directional control. An extremely talented driver like Art Chrisman's nephew Jack could get one of these cars down the track with great dexterity—and indeed he came close to winning the 1959 NHRA Nationals—but most drivers could not. The sidewinders soon disappeared, and for most of the 1960s the dominant design paradigm remained the single-engine slingshot.

With the Bustle Bomb, Lloyd Scott attacked the problem of horsepower and weight transfer to the rear wheels by carrying an Oldsmobile engine in front and a Cadillac behind him. This was the first dragster to top 150 mph.

THE BUG

1950

Dick Kraft built The Bug from a
vehicle once used to spray insecticide in orange groves.

Evolution of a Slingshot

In the early 1950s nobody had given much thought to designing a vehicle exclusively for acceleration, and there were a number of ways to go. One was to pare weight to a minimum, and among the first to do this was Dick Kraft, who converted a stripped-down Ford once used to spray orange groves into a drag racing machine. Called the Bug, it gave us the name "rail job" because it looked like an engine on rails.

Bob Rounthwaite's Thingie had the engine mounted high in front, raising the center of gravity to keep the rear tires from spinning excessively. Lightening a car while increasing power often diminished traction, slowing the acceleration.

Joaquin Arnett maximized weight transfer by locating the cockpit behind the rear axle. In a similar machine, the J. E. Riley Special, Calvin Rice won the first NHRA Nationals in 1955.

Mickey Thompson used a narrowed rear axle and a high degree of kingpin inclination in front, two keys to going straight when leaving the line. His dragster shot out "like a rock in a slingshot," said one witness.

The name stuck and the design attained an exquisite functionality in the Greer-Black-Prudhomme machine of the early 1960s.

The Greer-Black-Prudhomme machine was a *classic example of the slingshot design and was nearly unbeatable in its day.*

Anatomy of a Top Fuel Dragster

The modern, mid-engine design for dragsters evolved partly as a result of the continuing search for better weight transfer, and partly for safety reasons. With the engine in front, not only was a driver's vision restricted, but if an engine or transmission blew, the driver was liable to suffer serious injuries, either from flying parts or burning nitro, or both.

Although drivers like Ollie Morris, Tony Nancy, Jack Chrisman, and others had tried the design during the 1950s and '60s, none of them was successful enough to compel profound changes throughout the sport. Many of these machines were hard to control.

In drag racing, as elsewhere, necessity is the mother of invention. A series of serious mishaps involving slingshots in the early 1970s opened the door to innovation once again, and this time mid-engine dragsters roared to the top. Within a year or so of the first winning appearance of a mid-engine fueler, slingshots had all but disappeared from the drag strips. At a time when the biggest innovators at the tracks were the new Funny Cars, the mid-engine revolution rekindled fan interest in the fuelers. Prior to this time, the highest speeds attained by slingshots were in the 230 mph range. Mid-engine top speeds approached 250 mph by 1973, and have been climbing ever since.

Modern *Top Fuel dragsters like the Bill Miller Engineering machine, bottom and facing page, feature a rear-engine design that is not only safer for the driver but helps distribute weight better.*

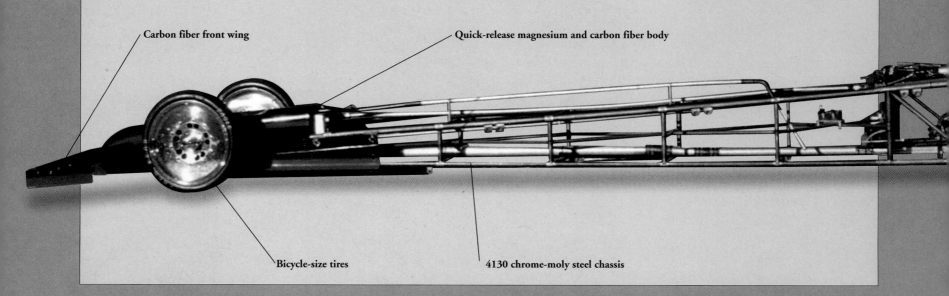

Carbon fiber front wing

Quick-release magnesium and carbon fiber body

Bicycle-size tires

4130 chrome-moly steel chassis

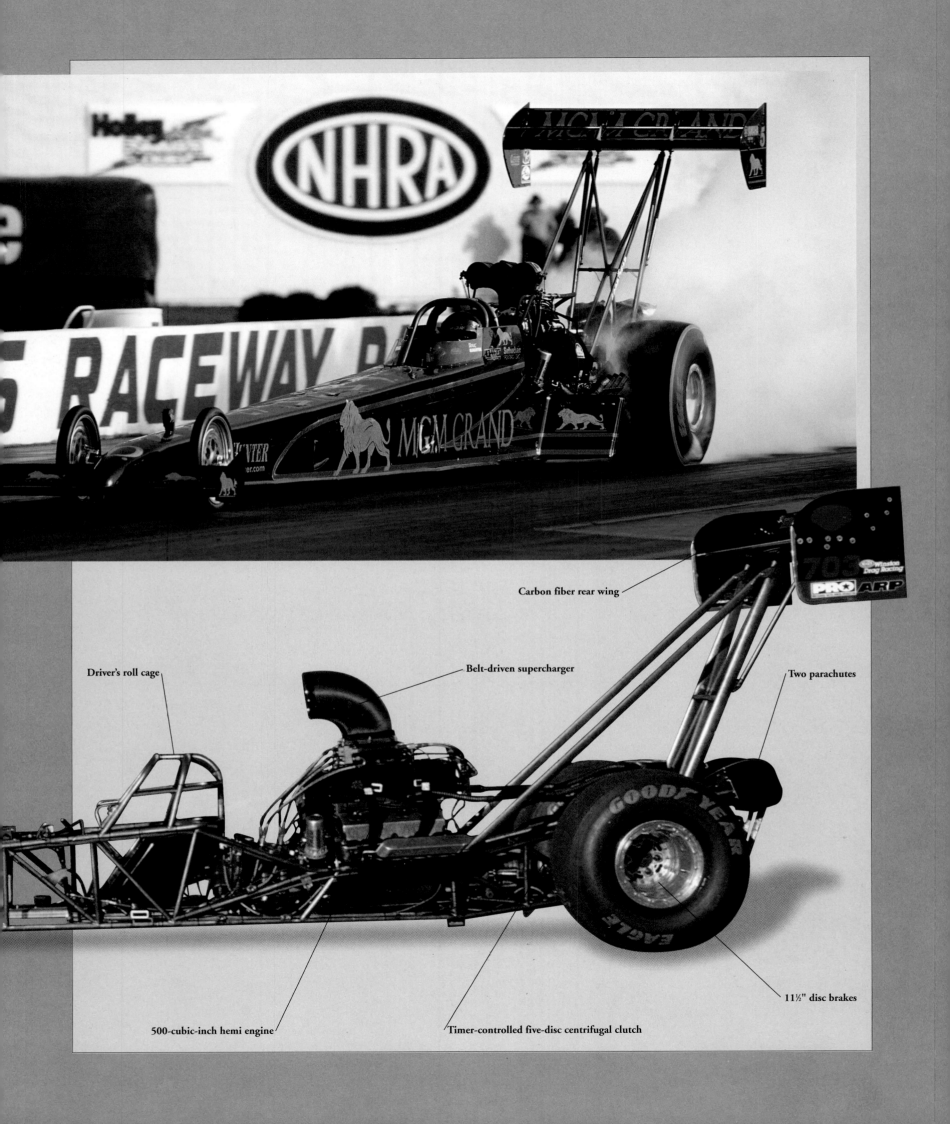

Carbon fiber rear wing

Belt-driven supercharger

Driver's roll cage

Two parachutes

11½" disc brakes

500-cubic-inch hemi engine

Timer-controlled five-disc centrifugal clutch

1964

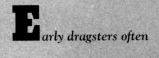

Early dragsters often emulated IndyCars (as with Melvin Heath's car at left) and Bonneville roadsters with streamlined bodies that enclosed the engines and chassis. The slingshot concept (car at right) put the driver's weight behind the wheels for maximum traction. Eventually bodies disappeared as racers recognized the advantages of a lightweight "rail" with a naked frame.

Prudhomme's nickname, "Snake," matched his uncanny reflexes and killer instinct. He dominated Funny Car racing in the mid-'70s with his army-sponsored cars, winning four consecutive championships. So popular was the Snake that millions of toy race cars immortalized his rivalry with friend and partner Tom "Mongoose" McEwen.

Don "Snake" Prudhomme

Don "Snake" Prudhomme's racing résumé is a long one, spanning a thirty-five-year driving career and his years since 1994 as owner of the U.S. Tobacco Co. Funny Car and the Miller Lite Top Fuel dragster.

Snake began his championship racing career in dragsters, winning forty-nine NHRA events across four decades. In the 1970s he became the first driver to win four NHRA Winston Series Funny Car championships. He drove the first Funny Car under six seconds (5.98 in 1975), was the first in the 5.60s, first under 5.20, and the first to break 250 mph. He was also the third Top Fuel dragster driver to break the 300 mph barrier, in 1983.

Top racers have a killer instinct, and Snake was at the pinnacle, winning his forty-nine events in sixty-eight final appearances. Overall, driver Don Prudhomme won 389 of 589 rounds of competition, for a .660 winning percentage.

As an owner, one of his best days was at the 1998 Winternationals, when both of his drivers, Ron Capps in the Funny Car and Larry Dixon Jr. in the dragster, won their events. Heading into the twenty-first century, Prudhomme-owned cars have won fifteen victories so far, with the promise of more to come.

Don Prudhomme made a smooth transition from driver to mentor, molding Funny Car racer Ron Capps, top, and Top Fuel driver Larry Dixon Jr., left, in his own image as personable and successful racers.

Snake Prudhomme
earned his winning reputation
in a Top Fuel dragster in the
'60s. He returned to his racing
roots at the end of his career,
winning three Top Fuel races in
his "Final Strike" farewell tour
in 1994.

"We had to fight for **survival**, no matter what it took, because we had to make enough money to go to the **next race.**"

—DON "SNAKE" PRUDHOMME, NHRA DRIVER/OWNER, ON THE EARLY DAYS

1955

SPONSORED BY
NATIONAL HOT ROD
ASSOCIATION

STAR
Nationa

Mickey Thompson, in the car at

right, wore many hats as an innovator, entrepreneur, promoter, and showman. He raced

anything with wheels, from slingshot dragsters and IndyCars to Funny Cars and off-road trucks.

MICKEY THOMPSON

Mickey Thompson is a name that is as much an emblem for the American automotive scene as Babe Ruth is for baseball. Thompson's involvement in auto racing included midget, sprint, and sports cars, drag racing, IndyCars, power boats, off-road racing, land speed record attempts, and more. He was successful as a driver, an innovator, and a promoter, and wherever the pulse of automotive engines and speed was felt, Mickey Thompson was there. He was the first American to drive faster than 400 mph, he holds 295 speed records at Bonneville alone, and his driving and design feats helped shape the American motorsports landscape.

Thompson was also deeply involved in off-road racing. He co-founded SCORE, developed wide oval tires and nitrogen gas shocks, and won championships in as many types of automotive racing as you can name. As a promoter, he helped popularize indoor racing in covered stadiums. Tires and wheels bearing his name are sold worldwide.

His involvement in drag racing began in the days of dry lakes racing, when he was too young to drive legally, as a racer at El Mirage. During his drag racing career, he was a slingshot dragster driver, was the first six-second Funny Car driver, was instrumental in helping develop directional stability in the slingshot dragster design, and experimented with streamlining and four-wheel-drive, as well. Two of Thompson's innovations can be seen in action today at any drag strip: the starting and foul light systems.

The Gasser Wars

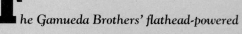

Willys Gassers (gas-fueled coupes) provided some of the most exciting competition from the late '50s to the mid-'60s. The Stone-Woods-Cook car of Fred Stone, Leonard Woods, and Doug "Cookie" Cook was among the strongest of the blown Gassers, though driver Cook always had trouble with "Ohio George" Montgomery, whose No. 269 was the first in a long line of dominant Gassers.

There were many exciting Gasser rivalries, but the most ballyhooed was the one between Doug Cook and Big John Mazmanian; the two are seen (opposite page, top) coming off the line together at Pomona. Pebble, Pulp, Chef, and Big June, as they were called, were featured in a long series of hilarious ads run by cam grinders Ed Iskenderian and Jack Engle. "Drag racing needed more color during the mid '60s," said John Mazmanian, and with the Gasser wars, drag racing was never more colorful.

The Gamueda Brothers' flathead-powered Anglia, top, and George Montgomery's '33 Malco Willys, bottom, were good examples of the Gassers that ran the strips during the '60s.

1967

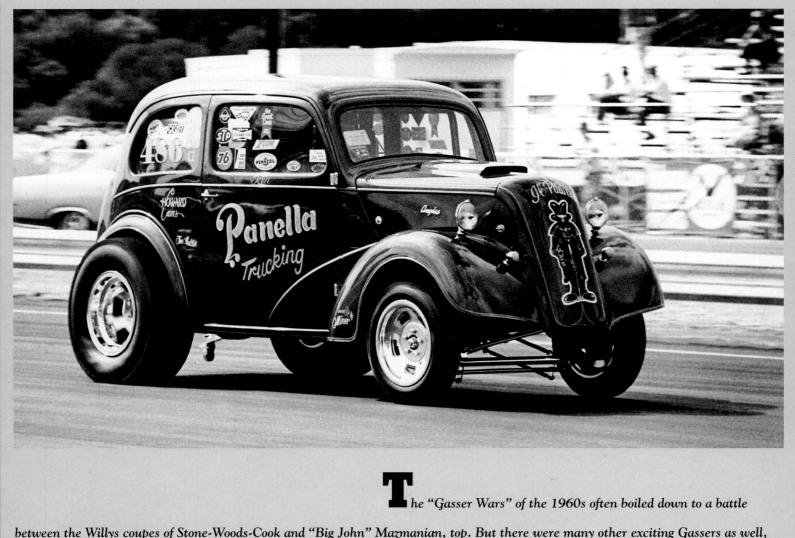

The "Gasser Wars" of the 1960s often boiled down to a battle between the Willys coupes of Stone-Woods-Cook and "Big John" Mazmanian, top. But there were many other exciting Gassers as well, such as the Panella Trucking Anglia driven by Ken Dondero, bottom.

The 1999 Pro Stock Motorcycle championship came down to the last day of the season, and Angelle Seeling lost out by eight points—the closest margin in the history of the class. She lost even though she had posted the best overall won-lost record, 33-9 (.786), and indeed the best throughout all the pro classes, save only for John Force's .847. Angelle fought back tears while congratulating Matt Hines in the Pomona shutoff, but she told herself that next time it would be different.

Angelle took her first ride on a motorcycle at age six. At twenty she began competing in the ET brackets at State Capital Dragway in Baton Rouge. In 1995, at twenty-five, she sailed through the Pro Stock Motorcycle course at Frank Hawley's Drag Racing School in Gainesville, her skills and determination capturing the imagination of her instructor, George Bryce. The next year she went to work as Bryce's rider on the NHRA circuit, won the fourth event she entered (the Keystone Nationals in Reading, Pennsylvania), and finished seventh in the point standings. In 1997 she was fifth, in 1998 second. And in 1999 she was second again, by that eight-point margin, after having qualified first four times, making the final round seven times, and leading the chase for most of the season. In 2000, Angelle finally broke through and won the Pro Stock Motorcycle Championship.

Angelle is a registered nurse, and may eventually return to that profession. But not quite yet. Already she stands near the top in NHRA in one regard: she is one of only two female competitors ever to have won ten or more professional victories. The other is Shirley Muldowney.

The man who edged out Angelle in 1999, Matt Hines, is the only rider to have won three times in a row, 1997–99, and all this before turning twenty-eight! Not that Matt's experience doesn't go deep. With partner Terry Vance (Vance & Hines Racing, Santa Fe Springs, California), Matt's father Byron has long been a dominant force in motorcycle drag racing. Young Matt won his first national event in 1996, in just his seventh try, and was named NHRA Rookie of the Year.

When he scored his first championship in 1997, with his father as crew chief, Matt was the second-youngest pro champ in NHRA history. In 1999, his Suzuki seemed to lower the speed and elapsed-time records at just about every event. The records stood at 7.154 and 191.48 at the end of the season, by which time his twenty-three national-event wins ranked him fourth all-time. And Matt's winning percentage of .837 was the best of any professional competitor in NHRA history.

While most race car drivers are surrounded by a cocoon of steel tubing, a Pro Stock Bike rider has only a helmet and leather suit for protection. Pro Stock Bike engines are among the most sophisticated powerplants in motorsports, producing more than 3 hp from each cubic inch of engine displacement.

Anatomy of a Pro Stock Bike

A Top Fuel dragster makes almost 3 hp per pound of weight, but a Pro Stock Bike is no slouch: 300 hp in a 600-pound two-wheeler. The four-cylinder engines—mostly Kawasakis or Suzukis—are limited to 1,508 cubic centimeters for two-valve configurations with eight spark plugs and 1,429 cc for four valves and four plugs. These high-revving engines have four carburetors and dual overhead cams. The seven-inch clutches have nine fiber disks and nine steel floaters.

Chrome-moly chassis are restricted to a 70-inch wheelbase, but wheelie bars—a critical component for tuning the chassis—can extend another 60 inches beyond the rear axle. Cloaking the chassis is an "aerodynamically enhanced"

Pro Stock Bike engines, below, are capable of revving over 13,500 revolutions per minute.

Pro Stock Bike's first dominant force was John Myers, facing page, top, who won three NHRA Winston championships in the 1990s.

Solid-mounted rear axle

Non-metallic casters   10" x 15" lightweight motorcycle slick   Carbon fiber fender

replica of a body that matches the engine. Atop the body is a two-step seat: After getting off the line, riders slide back from the lower portion to cut wind resistance and improve weight transfer. Ready to race, a Pro Stock Bike will cost about of $20,000 for the chassis with an aluminum fork, swing arm, handlebars, foot pegs, engine mount, and fuel tank (one-quart capacity); $25,000 for the engine; and as much as $10,000 for the on-board data recorder.

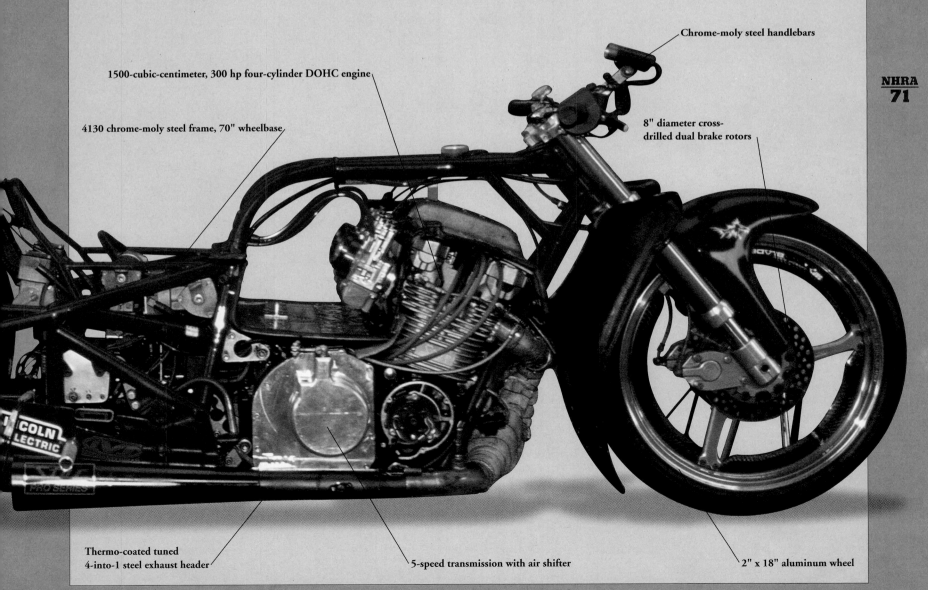

Chrome-moly steel handlebars

1500-cubic-centimeter, 300 hp four-cylinder DOHC engine

4130 chrome-moly steel frame, 70" wheelbase

8" diameter cross-drilled dual brake rotors

Thermo-coated tuned 4-into-1 steel exhaust header

5-speed transmission with air shifter

2" x 18" aluminum wheel

Exhibitionists

In a sense, every drag race car puts on an exhibition every time it runs down the track. In modern-day racing, nobody understands this better than Funny Car champion John Force, but from the beginning, certain racers were as attentive to "the show" as to going fast. The Bean Bandits had their peasant whites, Art Chrisman his impeccable chrome and lacquer. The long, smoky burnout was perfected by showmen like Jungle Jim Liberman and Farkonis, Coil, and Minnick, the team behind the unforgettable Chi-Town Hustler. Machines powered by hydrogen peroxide rockets enjoyed a brief vogue, but speeds

approaching 400 mph proved to be way too dangerous. So did the spectacular but dangerous fire burnouts, which were finally banned even though fans loved them.

Big Daddy Don Garlits could light things up pretty well, but a real master of the fire burnout was "TV Tommy" Ivo, who was arguably the greatest showman ever. Ivo was one of the first touring pros—he appeared at strips from coast to coast as early as 1960, and he was

certainly near the top in name recognition. His nickname stemmed from his movie and television career, notably as a character in the *My Little Margie* series. And in drag racing Ivo had established himself as a consummate exhibitionist before John Force was in his teens.

For sheer spectacle, Ivo never even came close to disappointing his fans. In his first years as a pro, he drove everything from street roadsters trailing foxtails to his unique Showboat, which boasted four Buick engines and four-wheel drive, and cost him $13,000 in 1960. Then he toured with a succession of immaculate and hard-charging fuel dragsters— one of which was the first ever to run in the fives, at a Pennsylvania strip in October 1972—often transporting his cars in a glass-sided trailer. Toward the end of his career, Tommy switched to fuel Funny Cars and in the early 1980s he fulfilled a longtime ambition by campaigning a jet dragster. Like the Showboat, jets were classified strictly as exhibition vehicles and were not allowed to run in NHRA competition, but their sound and power were always thrilling to fans.

As of the year 2000, jet dragsters and jet Funny Cars make up the largest group of exhibition machines, but other types are around as well. Bill "Maverick" Golden's Little Red Wagon, debuted in 1965, was the forerunner of a whole troupe of wheelstanders. Some of them are still on the scene, but none was ever a bigger fan favorite than Maverick's.

Little Red Wagon was designed to lift the wheels at the starting line and travel the length of the strip that way. The rear-engined Hemi Under Glass, opposite, put on a similar show, but Art Arfons' Green Monster, top opposite, and other jets like it started out as serious attempts at speed.

1960

1969

Jet cars like Green Monster and Walt Arfons' Smoky, top, were

banned by NHRA as unsafe. The Backup Pickup, bottom, was designed purely for shows like this one at Carlsbad in 1969. Tommy Ivo's

Showboat, opposite, with four Buick engines, couldn't match the times of single-engine dragsters but was a popular exhibition car.

Getting Up Speed

Conventional wisdom recognizes the Bug as a precursor to the modern dragster. It was a stripped-down jalopy whose sole purpose was to travel the quarter mile as quickly and efficiently as possible. Campaigned by Dick Kraft at Santa Ana Raceway in 1950, The Bug was little more than an engine stand on wheels. In the years since the Bug, cars have gotten much more sophisticated. They are no longer engine stands on wheels—more like cruise missiles between chrome-moly frame rails. They can reach speeds of 100 mph in a second, over 250 mph in three seconds, and 330 mph in four and a half seconds. Despite refinements in both the anatomy and propulsion systems of a dragster, two elements have remained constant: superchargers and nitromethane.

Fuel Funny Car art

Superchargers are one of the icons of drag racing. Called the "blower," or "wind machine," or "huffer," a supercharger's very shape has come to represent the sound and fury of the sport. Spinning at 12,000 rpm, this glorified air compressor force-feeds even more oxygen into an already volatile chemical situation with a fury that belies its tenor zing and whistle. It takes as much as 1,000 hp just to spin the rotors on these wind machines, more energy than an IndyCar produces. But the huge expenditure pays off: After supercharging, the fiercest and most prodigious of these fuel engines produce over 6,000 hp.

Now, gasoline is a fuel, but no way is it fuel. For drag racers and fans alike, fuel means just one thing: nitromethane. Every time a pair of nitro burners face off at a drag race, the flash of yellow and then green from the starting lights unleashes two chariots of fire.

$$CH_3NO_2$$
nitromethane

Pop. Cackle. Liquid Horsepower. Joy Juice. The Yellow Stuff. The Sweet and Sour Sauce. As acrid as it is punishing, when it reaches its flash point, nitromethane is an angry pit viper of a hydrocarbon and its practitioners are snake handlers who have taken it on faith that they won't get bitten—but they often do. Nitromethane is a monopropellant, which is a fancy way of saying that it carries its own oxygen, and therefore once it is lit or merely compressed, it is as volatile as a downed high-tension line dancing across the highway.

Nitro's racing history began with Italian rocket scientists as early as 1929, followed by Russian rocket design teams testing a combination of kerosene and a nitromethane derivative a year later. Streamlined Auto Union Grand Prix cars of the 1930s, running land speed record times on the autobahn, reached speeds of almost 270 mph running on nitro. After a mild batch of nitro helped catapult John Cobb to a speed of 403 mph at the Bonneville Salt Flats in his Railton Mobil special streamliner in 1947, it did not take long for other racers of the day to become converts. Nitro was a strange and forbidden fruit back then. Racers received it in drums marked "cleaning fluid," and one hot rodder was rumored to have "leached" it from used motion picture film. Despite its volatility, the energy, power, and torque from a super-charged, nitro-burning engine emerge only under certain conditions. It is as if the requirements for a nitro-powered engine to roar to life are as stringent and mysterious as those for life itself to arise in any given galaxy. The seemingly universal rules that apply to other, tamer fuels no longer apply in an engine fueled by nitromethane.

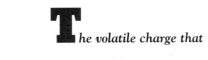

The volatile charge that makes nitro racing what it is can self-destruct as easily as it can destroy the competition.

Doug Herbert's
violent engine explosion at the
Pomona Raceway starting line
in November 1999 was the most
spectacular many had ever seen,
all the more so because Herbert
walked away unharmed. NHRA
instituted the 90 percent nitro
rule the following year, bringing
levels down from as much as
98 or 99 percent.

Drag racing in the 1990s marked the emergence of many second-generation racers in the nitro ranks, such as Top Fuel driver Tony Schumacher, son of Funny Car driver and team owner Don Schumacher.

How so? Nitro conducts electricity and can ground out the spark against the surface of the combustion chamber itself, triggering an explosion like a liquid fuse. Conversely, nitro can also extinguish the spark from a magneto that has enough amperage to work as an arc welder. When the spark has been snuffed, the fuel pouring into the cylinder rapidly begins "puddling," and on the compression stroke of the engine, the unburnt fuel is squeezed into a critical mass and detonates like a bomb.

As mind-boggling as the volatility of the stuff under pressure is the amount of it that is consumed during a quarter-mile run. Sid Waterman is a fuel pump manufacturer who designs pumps for both drag racers and race cars at the Indy 500. He said this about the amount of fuel needed to power a nitro burner down the drag strip: "If I took the [fuel] pump off of John Force's Funny Car and we put it out here in the center of the Indianapolis Speedway, and put out thirty-three hoses, I could run all thirty-three cars off the same fuel pump and still probably bypass something back to the tank."

> ## "The ground shakes,
> ### header flames six feet in the air, for one brief moment nothing else on Earth seems to matter."
> **—BOB HENKES, NHRA FAN, APPLE VALLEY, MINNESOTA**

A fuel car will consume nearly fifteen gallons of fuel in a single run, at a cost of $30 a gallon. And modern fuel racers discard pistons and crankshafts as casually as they discard spark plugs. A fuel engine costs about $30,000, so it's easy to see that 6,000 hp doesn't come cheap. But even though NHRA now restricts nitro mixtures to 90 percent, the apocalyptic roar is undiminished, and the fumes when a fueler is fired in the pits still send even seasoned fans running for cover. But it is that roar, those intoxicating fumes, and the 6,000 hp that fans love most. There is plenty of great drag racing without nitro, but if there were no nitro, the sport would be significantly diminished.

Among the great racing outside the fuel ranks is the Pro Stock division, NHRA's factory hot rods. These cars look much like the ones fans drive to the races, with doors that open and stock suspension, with the same roots as the fuel cars. In fact, it could be argued that the Bug was closer in spirit to a contemporary Pro Stocker, which still continues to use carburetors and gasoline, accessories that the more exotic Top Fuelers mothballed forty years ago.

Funny Car racing provides showmanship and audacity unmatched in any other category. Former Pro Modified champion Scotty Cannon helped raise the bar when he joined the Funny Car ranks in the late 1990s.

With all eight candles lit, there's no more dramatic scene in racing than a fuel car at twilight. Here you can almost feel the power of Jerry Toliver's Firebird "flopper" coming off the line with the butterflies wide open. The amount of fuel being forced into the cylinders is seven times the volume of water coming out of your shower head at home in the morning.

TONY SCHUMACHER

Tony Schumacher was born to drive fast. His father, Don "the Shoe" Schumacher, was a dominating Funny Car driver in his day, and Tony began NHRA drag racing at the age of nineteen in his Super Street Chevelle, a 90 mph car.

By 1992 he was racing a Super Comp dragster at NHRA events, where he was recruited by Wayne Knuth to drive a jet dragster around the country for exhibitions. Tony spent two years touring the drag strips of North America in that jet car, running nearly 300 mph. But that wasn't enough, and in 1995 Tony formed his own NHRA Alcohol Funny Car team,

driving a 250 mph Olds Achieva. He won his first NHRA major event with that car, but the next year it blew up and Tony was quickly recruited by Mike and Greg Peek to drive their Top Fuel dragster. He qualified in his first event, racing to the finals, and it was immediately clear that Tony had found a home in the cockpit of a Top Fueler.

Throughout 1997, Tony was a regular in the elimination rounds at NHRA events, but without the heavyweight sponsorship, the La Bac dragster just couldn't stay with the top winners. Halfway through the 1998 season Tony's father, Don, formed his own Top Fuel team with Exide Batteries

as sponsor and they signed Tony on to drive their brand-new dragster at the Nationals. He qualified in that brand-new car, and it was the beginning of big things to come, as Tony and the team went on to a dream season in 1999: the first dragster to break the 330 mph barrier and an NHRA Winston Top Fuel championship. Clearly this was only the beginning for Tony Schumacher. He first inherited his love for drag racing from his dad, and then he got the nickname: "the Shoe."

Tony Schumacher had driven the Army Top Fuel dragster into close contention for the top spot in NHRA Winston Drag Racing season points chase. But a crash at the AutoZone Nationals in Memphis, Tennessee, ended his season, and his bid to defend his Top Fuel championship in 2000.

50 Years of Speed Records

NHRA is the guardian of the sport of drag racing, having carefully guided its growth through the decades. But the racers themselves chart the course for technology and

Pro Stock Bike
Year	Racer	MPH
1980	TERRY VANCE	151.26
1986	TERRY VANCE	163.51
1989	JOHN MAFARO	170.90
1994	JOHN MYERS	180.00
1999	ANTRON BROWN	190.70

Pro Stock
Year	Racer	MPH
1982	WARREN JOHNSON	181.08
1986	WARREN JOHNSON	190.07
1997	WARREN JOHNSON	200.13

Top Fuel
Year	Racer	MPH
1962	CONNIE KALITTA	180.36
1963	DON GARLITS	190.26
1964	DON GARLITS	201.34
1965	DENNY MILANI	211.26
1966	DON COOK	223.32
1967	JAMES WARREN	230.17
1973	DON GARLITS	
1975	DON GARLITS	
1984	JOE AMATO	
1986	DON GARLITS	
1987	JOE AMATO	
1989	CONNIE KALITTA	
1992	KENNY BERNSTEIN	
1994	KENNY BERNSTEIN	
1997	CORY McCLENATHAN	
1999	TONY SCHUMACHER	

Funny Car
Year	Racer	MPH
1968	GENE SNOW	200.44
1982	DON PRUDHOMME	
1984	KENNY BERNSTEIN	
1986	KENNY BERNSTEIN	
1987	MIKE DUNN	
1991	JIM WHITE	
1993	JIM EPLER	
1996	CRUZ PEDREGON	
1998	JOHN FORCE	

MPH   150   160   170   180   190   200   210   220   230

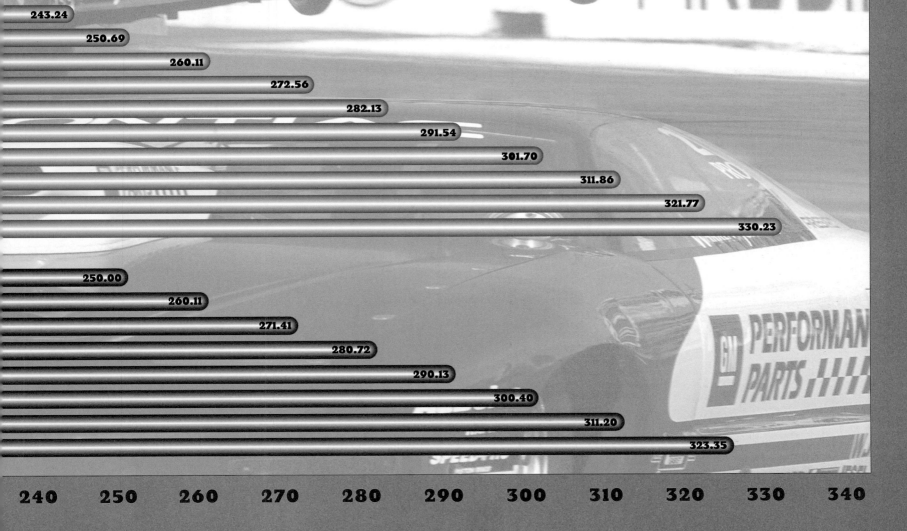

innovation in a relentless pursuit of speed. To a drag racer, there's no such thing as too fast. Over the last fifty years they've spent countless hours poring over data, tweaking this and tuning that, with success often measured in fractions of miles per hour or thousandths of a second. Whenever a racer succeeded, the bar got raised and everyone went back to work to top it, whether it was Don Garlits' Top Fuel firsts in the 200s or Kenny Bernstein breaking what many believe to be drag racing's last great barrier, 300 mph.

243.24
250.69
260.11
272.56
282.13
291.54
301.70
311.86
321.77
330.23

250.00
260.11
271.41
280.72
290.13
300.40
311.20
323.35

240   250   260   270   280   290   300   310   320   330   340

Burnouts

For many years, fuel cars typically poured smoke off the slicks as they left the start, and sometimes all the way to the finish line. In the late 1960s came the realization that spinning the tires was killing elapsed times and that it would be far better to get the tires hooked up and to confine slippage to the clutch. And so a new type of clutch, the "slider," became part of the conventional package and evolved into the multiple-stage units developed by Lanny and Tony Miglizzi and Bob Brooks, among others.

Of course, cars still pour smoke off the tires—having rolled through a water trough behind the starting line—but only as a preliminary to the actual run, to heat the rubber and enhance traction. That's the ideal, anyway. Misjudge the clutch setup or the condition of the track and you'll go up in smoke at

some point during the run, which usually means a wasted qualifying effort or a race lost.

Burnouts are partly a matter of enhancing traction, and partly a matter of show. Some drivers, particularly in the Top Fuel ranks, have found that going only a couple of hundred feet is sufficient. But some fuel Funny Car shoes go much farther, and there are times—especially in match races—when a car will

coast all the way to the lights after a burnout. Truly necessary for performance? Probably not, but then, "performance" can be theatrical as well as technological. Burnouts were largely responsible for establishing the popularity of Funny Cars in the first place, and to this day you will find hardly any fan who doesn't think that a big smoker isn't at least as exciting as a 300 mph charge down the track, hooked up and smokeless.

The sight and sound of a good burnout is unforgettable. The machines disappear into a wall of dense white smoke, as drivers keep the pedal to the metal until they are as much as halfway down the strip.

Everyone is there to win, and a good burnout at the right time is part of a winning combination. But the right time is before the race, when burnouts heat and clean the tires as well as build up the stickum on the track. A good burnout can be the most memorable thing about a race to some fans, but once the light tree goes green, drivers all agree it's better to run smokeless and win than to spin the wheels 60 feet from the start and lose.

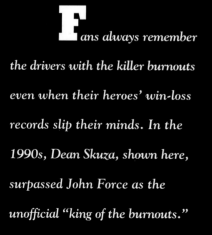

Fans always remember
the drivers with the killer burnouts
even when their heroes' win-loss
records slip their minds. In the
1990s, Dean Skuza, shown here,
surpassed John Force as the
unofficial "king of the burnouts."

Canadian Gary Beck
smoked his American rivals regularly, winning
nineteen national events and two Top Fuel
championships. Beck's first victory was perhaps
his biggest: He won the 1972 U.S. Nationals
in his Top Fuel debut.

John Force thrills
fans by keeping his foot in it way
past the 660-foot mark on some
of his burnouts.

BILL "GRUMPY" JENKINS

If Bill "Grumpy" Jenkins ever tries to tell you he wasn't all that good a driver, don't listen to him. But if he just wants to talk racing, soak up every word. In the early days, Jenkins started out in the business as an engine builder for other drivers like Dave Strickler. As a driver himself, he won the 1965 Winternationals Top Stock championship in his first national event. He went on to race an A/S Chevy II with a small-block engine and then moved to the Super Stock class and won the 1967 Nationals.

But the handicapped starts of Super Stock evolved into fuel Funny Car racing, and the increasing costs and dangers of racing these cars, as well as the potential of product identification with Detroit models, led Jenkins and a number of other top drivers like Ronnie Sox and

Bill Jenkins was one of the founding fathers of Pro Stock, winning legions of Chevrolet fans with his wheelstanding Camaros. Educated as an engineer, Jenkins brought a scientific approach to the sport.

Don Nicholson to approach NHRA with a new idea: the Pro Stock class.

In the first Pro Stock season —1970—Jenkins won the first two races and then hit a dry streak. But in 1972 he returned to the winner's circle in a revolutionary 327 Vega, defeating the Chrysler hemis to win the Winternationals. He went on to the NHRA championship that year, was nearly undefeated in match races, and grossed more money than most racers had heard of until then.

Jenkins revolutionized Pro Stock with his *invicible small-block Vega in 1972, above. Four years later, Larry Lombardo won the championship with a Jenkins-prepared Monza.*

Grumpy climbed out of the driver's seat a few years later and ran the racing team that won the 1976 NHRA Winston Championship with Larry Lombardo driving for Jenkins Competition.

Today Bill Jenkins has come full circle, building engines for Pro Stock Truck racers like Larry Kopp, who drove one of his engines to the NHRA Winston Championship in 1998.

Anatomy of a Pro Stock Car

Carbon fiber/Kevlar roof

Steel quarter panels

14" adjustable spoiler

NHRA
102

Solid-mounted titanium wheelie bars

33" x 17" x 15" slicks

15" x 15" aluminum wheels

Pro Stockers are NHRA's factory hot rods, cars that bear a certain resemblance to their showroom counterparts—they have doors that open and close, headlights that look like they work, stock suspension systems, and engines that are restricted to carbs and pump gas. They also turn speeds above 200, with ETs in the 6.80s. Pro Stock competition is so tight that only a few hundredths of a second separate the top qualifier from the bubble, and races sometimes appear to be dead heats.

NHRA rules specify bodies that must conform to templates based on factory specs, wheelbases from 103 to 106 inches, and a minimum weight of 2,350 pounds, driver included, which is only 25 pounds heavier than a fuel Funny Car. Most body panels are carbon fiber, the exception being the steel rear quarter panels and usually the

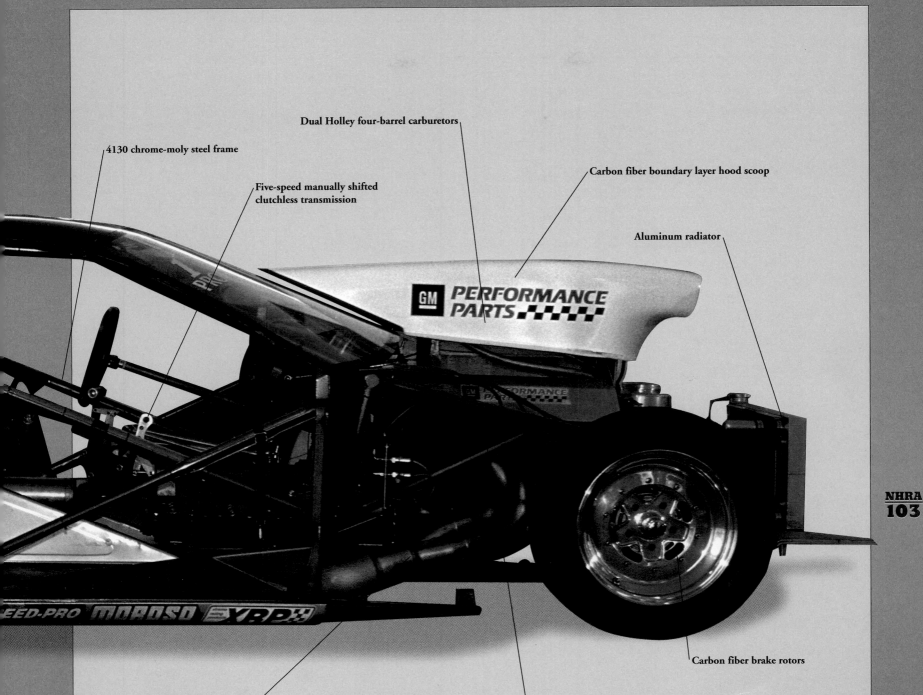

4130 chrome-moly steel frame

Dual Holley four-barrel carburetors

Five-speed manually shifted clutchless transmission

Carbon fiber boundary layer hood scoop

Aluminum radiator

GM PERFORMANCE PARTS

Stainless steel headers

500-cubic-inch, 1300 hp V-8 engine with cast iron block and aluminum cylinder heads

Carbon fiber brake rotors

roof. Spoilers are aluminum and chassis are 4130 chrome-moly, just as with the fuel cars. Even though a Top Fueler has nearly three times the wheelbase, a Pro Stocker requires 100 feet more tubing due to the complexity of the chassis layout and roll cage. The basic package costs about $75,000. And to field a competitive Pro Stocker? As long-time Pro Stock driver and owner Warren Johnson puts it: "An absolute minimum expenditure of $3 million," plus $1.5 million "to run one car for one year."

Pro Stock cars are anything but "showroom stock."

If fans know only one name from Pro Stock in the 1990s, it's probably Warren Johnson. "W. J.," "the Professor"—whatever you call him, he has taken his place alongside Bob Glidden and John Force as one of the winningest drivers of all time.

"Staging battles? I'm not aware of any staging battles. I just go in when I'm ready."

In the early 1970s the racing team of David Reher and Buddy Morrison, with Lee Shepherd behind the wheel, came out of Texas like a whirlwind to dominate the Sportsman classes at dozens of small drag strips across Texas and Oklahoma. By 1974 they won the Winternationals with an F/Gas Maverick wrapped around a Chevy engine. Another Modified win at the 1975 Springnationals followed, but by this time the team had their eyes on Pro Stock.

A crash at the 1976 Summernationals left Lee shaken but uninjured, and he quit racing for two years, only to return in 1978 to drive the Reher-Morrison Z28. The longer wheelbase felt safer to Shepherd, and his returned confidence led, in 1980, to a dominating season. Shepherd won six events and finished second three times out of ten NHRA national events, just missing the season championship. But that was just the beginning.

Shepherd won six more events the next year, and the team claimed their first NHRA Winston championship. New Pro Stock rules in 1982 gave the Reher-Morrison team added advantage, it seemed, as the Shepherd-driven cars continued to win. From 1980 through 1984, Lee Shepherd made the finals in forty-four out of the fifty-six events he entered. He won every NHRA tour race at least once, and compiled a 173-47 record in the Pro and Sportsman classes. Tragically, Lee Shepherd was killed in an accident while testing a car in Ardmore, Oklahoma, in 1985, but was still named Pro Stock Driver of the Year that year for the fourth consecutive time.

Lee Shepherd was a soft-spoken Texan who let his four Pro Stock championships do his talking for him.

RICHIE STEVENS

Richie had gone to the drags with his dad, Richie Sr., a Sportsman racer, ever since he could remember. More than anything he wanted to drive, and in 1992—when barely a teenager—his dream began to come true: He took his first ride in a Jr. Dragster. It was obvious right off that he had the right stuff. By 1996 Richie had graduated to a Pro Stocker owned by the legendary Roy

Hill, and in 1997 he drove for Hill when Pro Stock Trucks debuted as NHRA exhibition vehicles. The next year he stepped back into a Pro Stocker, won the Winston Finals in Pomona (the youngest Pro Stock winner ever), and finished ninth in the points standings. In 1999 it got better: He went to three consecutive final rounds, won at the Mopar Parts Nationals in Englishtown, became the eighth member of the Speed-Pro 200 mph Pro Stock Club,

and moved up to fifth in the standings, just behind two-time champ Jim Yates.

With that kind of momentum, nobody doubts that it will get even better than that for Richie Stevens. Although he turned twenty-two in 2000, Richie is still "the Kid" to his fellow Pro Stock racers—the first driver to move from Jr. Dragsters into the top professional ranks. Nobody doubts that there will be plenty of others.

Richie "the Kid" Stevens has shot down many veterans of Pro Stock with his gunfighter reflexes at the starting line. A graduate of NHRA's Jr. Dragster Program, Stevens has both youth and experience on his side.

the class that soon morphed into fuel Funny Cars. His Eliminator I, the first tube-framed flopper, was also first in the sevens.

Don's pioneering endeavors were far from over. In 1969, along with Ronnie Sox and Bill Jenkins, he put together a Super Stock match-racing program, and these cars soon morphed into Pro Stockers. And, once again, Don was the first to put one of them into the sevens. In 1977 he mounted an all-out effort and won the Pro Stock championship, defeating both Bob Glidden and Warren Johnson by hefty margins. An early convert to the nostalgia movement, "Dyno" campaigned a 7.50-second '62 Chevy bubbletop on into the 1990s, and in the latter '90s he was one of the first with a Pro Stock Truck. The century ended with Don in his seventies, but don't rule him out quite yet. With tricks up his sleeve for half a century or more, he may still have a few left.

"Dyno Don" got his nickname from his artistry in running a chassis dynamometer facility for a Chevrolet dealer in Pasadena, California (where he also had a big reputation as a street racer). Don, one of drag racing's fifty-year men, turned the first-ever 120 mph time, at Santa Ana in the summer of 1950 in the '34 Ford roadster he raced with brother Harold. A decade later, he got serious about Chevy stockers, and won Stock Eliminator at the 1961 Winternationals in a 409 Impala. A few years after that, he pioneered with a Mercury Factory Experimental,

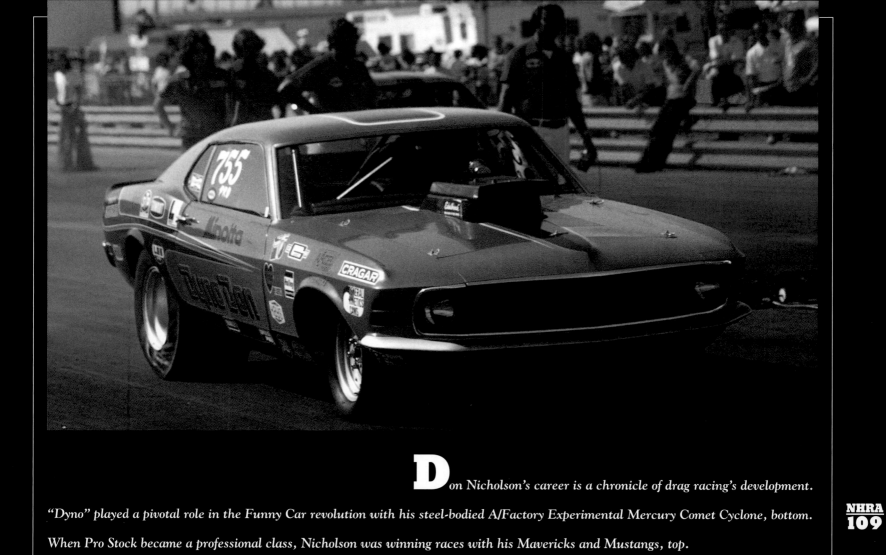

Don Nicholson's career is a chronicle of drag racing's development. "Dyno" played a pivotal role in the Funny Car revolution with his steel-bodied A/Factory Experimental Mercury Comet Cyclone, bottom. When Pro Stock became a professional class, Nicholson was winning races with his Mavericks and Mustangs, top.

BOB GLIDDEN

When Bob Glidden burst on the scene with a runner-up finish to Grumpy Jenkins in his first Pro Stock event at the 1972 NHRA Supernationals, few thought it was much more than a fluke. Certainly no one dreamed that this young man would go on to become NHRA's all-time winner with eighty-five victories, a mark that would go unsurpassed until John Force did it in 2000.

But Bob Glidden came back to win the NHRA Nationals in 1973 and 1974, the NHRA Winston Pro Stock championship in 1975, and kept winning with every car he drove. With a family team consisting of his wife, Etta, and his sons Billy and Rusty, the racer from Indiana made the NHRA U.S. Nationals at Indianapolis his own private event, winning seven more times there. He won an unheard-of ten NHRA Winston Championship titles.

Faced with rule changes in 1978 that caused him to decide to race a gigantic Ford Fairmont because it had an advantageous weight break, Glidden swept through a championship season. He switched from Ford to Chrysler the next year, a situation that usually requires racers to spend a half or full season just ironing out the kinks. Not Bob Glidden. He drove his new Plymouth Arrow into the winner's circle on his first time out at the 1980 Winternationals and set a new NHRA record along the way.

During the first fifty years there have been a number of family racing teams in NHRA, but none has been as successful and long-running as the Glidden team.

obody worked harder or won more Pro Stock races than Bob Glidden. A former line mechanic at a Ford dealership, he was worshipped by the Ford faithful, who forgave his brief flings with Chrysler and GM products. Bob proved he could win with any body style, from pint-size Pintos and sleek Thunderbirds, opposite top, to boxy Fairmonts, opposite bottom.

KENNY BERNSTEIN

"KB" is the only driver to have won world championships in both fuel Funny Cars and Top Fuel dragsters. He did it four times in a row in a Funny Car, 1985–1988, and once (so far) in Top Fuel, in 1996. Along the way, he has set countless records, including the first 300-mph run, on March 2, 1992, at Gainesville Raceway. Only Bob Glidden, John Force, and Warren Johnson have exceeded his fifty-three pro victories, thirty in Funny Cars, the others in Top Fuel. In nineteen years in the fuel classes, his average finish in the points chase, 3.6, is a mark nobody else approaches.

And certainly not the least of his attainments is his two-decade-plus Budweiser sponsorship, the longest-running in NHRA history.

Through his prowess at cultivating and sustaining sponsor support, KB has brought drag racing to a whole new level.

David Kimble

Under the skin of Kenny Bernstein's Ford Tempo Funny Car beat the heart of a Top Fuel dragster—a supercharged, nitro-burning hemi. Bernstein and crew chief Dale Armstrong terrorized their competition with breakthroughs in aerodynamics, clutch management, and fuel system technology.

"We took our vacation five seconds at a time."
—Kenny Bernstein, NHRA driver

SOX AND MARTIN

Top race car drivers are often called "shoes," but in the case of Ronnie Sox in the days of manually shifted race cars, it was his hands that set him apart. Teamed with businessman and promoter Buddy Martin in the 1960s and '70s, Ronnie Sox became a feared competitor. The Sox and Martin team first came onto the scene driving Cheverolet 409s and 427s, but they scored big when they teamed with Plymouth in 1965. Driving one of the original altered wheelbase A/FX Plymouths, they recorded the first nine-second runs for a normally aspirated doorslammer, and came close to finishing the year undefeated.

The classiest act in Pro Stock was clean-cut Buddy Martin and driver Ronnie Sox, the acknowledged king of four-speeds.

They ran a Barracuda Funny Car in 1966 and then moved to the new NHRA Super Stock Eliminator class the next season, where they continued their success. When NHRA created the Pro Stock category in 1970, Sox and Martin won three of seven national events that year, and six of eight the next.

People often say that the car makes the driver, but no one will ever say that about Ronnie Sox. He built his remarkable record in the days of four-speed manual shifters, and when racing moved to the Lenco clutchless transmissions by 1973, other drivers gained up to three-tenths of a second in their times. Sox saw his times drop by three to four hundredths. The new cars couldn't match his skill as a shifter.

Buddy Martin, the businessman and promoter of the team, still keeps in touch with drag racing as a consultant to the Pro Stock Truck team of Randy Daniels.

1966

Anatomy of a Pro Stock Truck

Pro Stock Trucks are like their automobile-bodied counterparts in that they bear some resemblance to what's seen in dealer showrooms: Dodge Dakotas, Chevy S-10s, and Ford Rangers. But they are also a lot different. While frames are 4130 chrome-moly, most of the body panels are steel, not carbon fiber, and the engines are not the same at all. Rather than 500-cubic-inch big-blocks, the engines are small-block V-8s with 358 cubes, the same size used in Winston Cup stock cars and the World of Outlaws sprinters. NHRA's aim is to enable the best use of existing technology and to

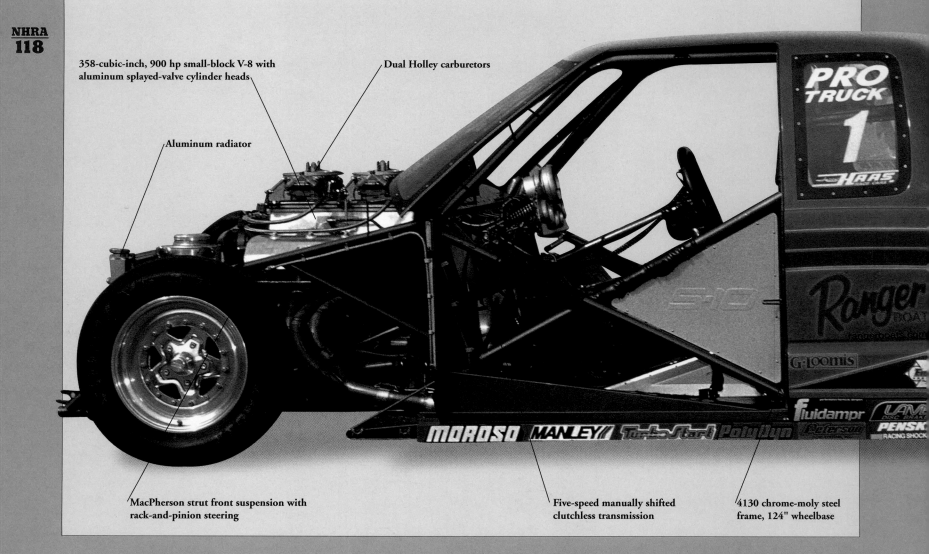

358-cubic-inch, 900 hp small-block V-8 with aluminum splayed-valve cylinder heads

Dual Holley carburetors

Aluminum radiator

MacPherson strut front suspension with rack-and-pinion steering

Five-speed manually shifted clutchless transmission

4130 chrome-moly steel frame, 124" wheelbase

keep costs affordable. And this aim has clearly been realized: More than forty trucks often show up for national events. They clock speeds in the 180s and 7.40 ETs, not quite what the Pro Stock cars are capable of, but nonetheless impressive to the huge numbers of NHRA fans who likewise drive Dakotas, S-10s, and Rangers.

Steel bed with flat cover

Single parachute

Solid-mounted wheelie bars

33" x 17" x 15" slicks

The cockpit of a Pro Stock Truck, top, is a spartan workplace surrounded by a spiderweb of steel tubing. Pro Stock Truck drivers shift for themselves with manual five-speed transmissions.

The Pro Stock Truck class emerged as a hot new class in NHRA racing, partly because it matched models that resemble those in the parking lot. Unlike the vintage model, below, which was probably driven right off the street to race in the early days, Pro Stock Trucks like Todd Patterson's Dodge, right, boast an aerodynamic body and a 358-cubic-inch engine that produces over 900 horsepower running on aviation gasoline. The fuel system on a truck like this flows at 7½ gallons per minute.

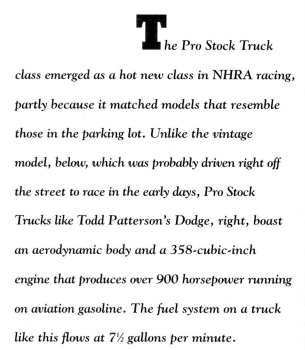

the trucks with an outstanding record in Comp Eliminator: thirteen national event wins and first in the sixes. Here, too, he was immediately successful: After the exhibition season in 1997, he finished second in the points standings in 1998. Although he slipped out of contention in 1999, nobody doubted that John would be a strong contender for the title in 2000 and beyond.

The two keys, he says, are "hard work on the performance side" and "a winning attitude," and he is certainly well proven on both accounts.

John Lingenfelter won fame in the Sportsman classes with a series of record-setting Super Stocks and dragsters. He was one of the first Sportsman stars to see the potential of the Pro Stock Truck class.

Pro Stock Truck has proved especially appealing to Sportsman competitors who see the class as a way of breaking into the pro ranks without the high costs of the other classes. John Lingenfelter came to

Suits and Chutes

One is a precaution, the other a necessity. Both are central to drag racing imagery, the head-to-toe fire-resistant outfits drivers wear, and the parachutes that blossom as cars clear the lights. Something had to be done to protect drivers in case of fire. Something also had to be done about enabling cars to come to a safe stop at strips that had been plenty long for 150 mph but were pretty short for 180. One solution was to add parachutes to supplement brakes.

One of the first to use a parachute was Mickey Thompson, who was familiar with these devices from Bonneville. They were enormous ring-slots, purchased as government surplus. Southern Californian Jim Deist was first to get into the manufacture of specialized chutes, and firesuits as well; he was soon joined by racer Bill Simpson and others. Today's Nomex firesuits will protect drivers from a conflagration of incredible intensity, and crossform chutes will slow them from the end of the quarter in an even shorter time than it takes to get there.

When pioneer strips like Pomona opened nearly fifty years ago, nobody was going much faster than 130. Now, drag racing has seen 330s, and yet Pomona is exactly the same length as it has always been. What has been achieved in braking technology is almost as impressive as what makes for those 330s.

*W*hat the well-dressed Funny Car driver, right, wore, circa 1972: a multilayered firesuit, aluminized gloves and boots, and a full face mask with filters. The first braking chutes were actually army surplus cargo chutes adapted to another heavy-duty purpose, below.

Driver Dave Braskett sits in the safety cage of his 1970 Camaro Funny Car in one of the fire-resistant suits of the early 1970s, including helmet, goggles, gas mask, aluminized gloves, and boots. The gloves were bulky, and the mask hindered vision nearly as much as the air intake on the supercharger, but protective garb was to evolve quickly.

"When you come
to the line
you bring your best game
or go
home."
—STEVE COBUN, NHRA FAN, ELDERSBURG, MARYLAND

One of the first important safety measures taken as speeds increased was the use of parachutes to help brake cars after the finish line. Those first heavy cargo chutes gave way to specially made drag chutes, left, with air slots to reduce the shock and G-forces of the sudden deceleration. In his early-'70s protective garb Tom McEwen, below, wore bulky aluminized gloves and face protection that resembled an old gas mask.

Racing Hearts

Many drag strip pundits consider a drag race a quarter-mile litmus test: an experiment to demonstrate the level of one's muster, engineering skill, and heart—especially heart. But it's not all as simple as winners and losers. A win light by itself is no measure of spunk and desire. In a discipline where there are fifteen losers and only one winner on any given Sunday, the payoff has to be more than just getting bathed by flashbulbs in the winner's circle and then cashing the check.

Every time drag racers suit up or grab a wrench or pack a parachute, they exhale and dig deep into their souls. They know—win or lose—that the real reward has to be the journey itself, a journey that leads to another opportunity to make smoke, noise, and fire.

There is comfort in this simple notion. It's the carrot that dangles in front of all drag racers, whether at the finish line, in an airport terminal, or on the interstate. In addition to their being mechanics, metallurgists, aerodynamic engineers, and human cannonballs, the trials and triumphs of drag racing also require racers to become philosophers. Without a fine-tuned sense of ulterior value in the face of adversity, they wouldn't have the gumption to stare down the starting-line Christmas Tree. Not that they aren't crushed when they lose, but they remain reflective. "That's what

"I'm gonna do this until I drop because I absolutely love it."
—JOHN FORCE, NHRA FUNNY CAR DRIVER

*T*op Fuel NHRA speed records up to James Warren's 230 mph in 1967 were set in front-engine dragsters.

I try to tell my guys when we were having a little down luck," one Funny Car driver said. "It seemed like luck. It seemed like, 'Why can't we do this?' There was always a little mistake here, a little mistake there. I told them, 'Maybe you should think about it like I think about it and that will help you deal with this a little bit. That car that's sitting there, it doesn't exist—you must understand that. It's an extension of your mind. It's an extension of you. A cylinder head just disappears when you talk about it because every part on the car is an extension of you. Every part on the car that comes out because it failed, you've failed.'"

The soul of the machine and the heart of the competitor seem like two sides of the same coin. Just as there are stress failures related to the tremendous loads these machines must endure, the heart and temperament of human beings also have very real frailties.

"Nowadays," one Funny Car tuner explained, "when you've got five or six guys on the team to travel all across the country with these cars, when you get different personalities, different egos and all that involved—that makes it a lot tougher. I mean, you know when you are the crew chief or the boss of these guys, you got to be a psychiatrist, a psychologist, a dad, the whole works."

Reconciling the heart with the mind is a balancing act. And keep in mind that

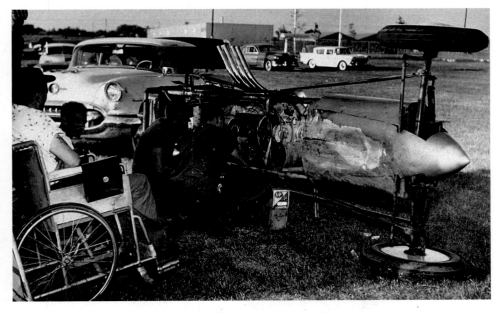

The modern pit area, top, is a far cry from the old days. Today fans can crowd around the cars to talk to their heroes between races. Four decades ago Raymond Godman, left, watched as crewmen worked on his Tennessee Boll Weevil dragster under primitive conditions in near-isolation. Godman competed for nearly thirty years in various classes while confined to a wheelchair as a result of injuries he sustained in Korea.

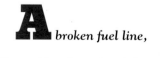 broken fuel line, top, causes starter Buster Couch to signal the driver to cut off the engine. The moment a driver has trouble, the NHRA Safety Safari, right, is on the scene, often arriving before the car has come to a stop.

"balance" is not normally associated with the personalities of drag racers. "Certifiable" is an adjective more than one racer might use to describe themselves. The struggle is to let the flame burn blue to stoke their sense of competition, but to avoid the white heat that consumes everything, including, possibly, the driver. One Top Fuel shoe explained the difference between good judgment and competitive fire this way: "I know how to drive and pack the parachute and mix nitro. And I try to stay away from mixing nitro because I just assume you pour straight nitro in it."

How do racers appease their innate desire to "tip the can" when it means possible annihilation? An analyst could conclude that professional drag racers are mad chemists with the hearts of firestarters. It's not easy to understand what makes them light a fire every ninety minutes—and set themselves in the eye of the inferno. It is the sign of very unusual individuals, and a drag race is in part a celebration not just of creativity and technology, but of certain dark impulses that lurk inside all of us.

Another Funny Car driver describes the slippery slope that is drag racing, a trajectory from infatuation to passion and devotion to compulsion and obsession: "You eat a pickle and you get a case of heartburn, you stop eating them—that's not an addiction. You go out there and blow your car up, you can't make your house payment for a couple of years, and you go out there and do it again—that's an addiction."

Call it addiction or dedication, all devotees need support groups, which explains the camaraderie among competitors who, once they are suited up, will try to race each other into the asphalt. On any Sunday, membership in this tribe can grow to sixty thousand, as race fans have the same passion as the racers themselves. It is a passion quenched only by the face-to-face showdowns of their drag racing heroes.

The plumes of fire and the haze of smoke connect many bleacher bums to an adolescence spent in the garage, polishing and tinkering with the family grocery getter, dreaming of the opportunity to wow both racers and race fans with their heart and prowess. And those fans not taken back to youthful dreams are analyzing and dissecting tune-ups as well as the reflexes and shrewdness of the drivers, confident that if they were either driving or tuning (or both), Top Eliminator would be theirs.

A day at the drag races brings with it a sense of belonging to an exclusive society. The members-only handshake can be as simple as an exchange of cash for a grandstand seat, or as advanced as mortgaging any semblance of a normal life for a career in drag racing.

But regardless of status or role, the drivers, teams, officials, and fans are merely capillaries in a much larger pulmonary system whose heart is the drive for excellence and the pursuit of horsepower. The heart of drag racing is bigger than the sum of its parts and it grows larger with the perseverance of its members.

In fifty years, NHRA drag racing has become a family sport that has spawned second-, third-, and even a few fourth-generation drivers.

1967

Linda Vaughn, the first lady of auto racing, has been an ambassador for the sport since she first appeared as Miss Hurst Golden Shifter in the 1960s. Her rapport with fans and racers is unrivaled to this day.

Thrilling millions of fans all over the globe is all in a day's work for World Wrestling Federation superstar "Stone Cold" Steve Austin, but sitting in the cockpit of Jerry Toliver's WWF Funny Car was enough to turn even Austin into an awestruck kid.

John Force and Co.

Fans have gotten used to the Funny Car speed and ET records being held by one person, the same guy who has dominated Funny Car racing as nobody else has dominated any professional class: John Force.

Force utterly ruled the 1990s, winning the championship every year except for 1992 when Cruz Pedregon edged him out. It's easy to forget that he never won a major event until 1987, or that he lost nine consecutive final rounds before winning. Before that, when he called his car Brute Force, his engine mishaps gained him a reputation as a "leaker." Though he had managed a top-ten finish in 1979, things didn't turn around for Force until 1984 when he hired Austin Coil.

Coil had been part of the team that made Chi-Town Hustler the most feared match-racer in the land, as well as a two-time NHRA champ in 1982 and 1983 with Frank Hawley in the seat.

Even with Coil, things didn't turn around at once. For five years, Force ranged from third to fifth in the standings. At one point he wasn't sure whether Kenny Bernstein could ever be dislodged from his perennial perch on top. When it happened in 1989, it was Bruce Larson, not Force, who did it. But beginning in 1990, Force could not be denied; one year he won thirteen events when no other competitor won more than one.

Eventually Force added a second car to his operation, driven by Tony Pedregon, his only serious competitor and younger brother of Cruz Pedregon, the only man to deprive him of the championship since 1990. Between them, Force and Pedregon owned all ten of the quickest and fastest Funny Car runs in NHRA history. Force hired a second crew chief, Larry Frazier, and a third, John Medlen. Take his over-the-top interview style, his tales of having been a truck driver and of having "seen Elvis at 1,000 feet," add his specialists and his dominance on the quarter mile, and you have the most famous, most popular, and most successful of all drag racers. At the turn of the twenty-first century in NHRA, John Force is The Man.

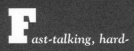 ast-talking, hard-driving John Force assembled a brain trust of crew chiefs who helped him win more races than any driver in NHRA history. Force is quick to credit Austin Coil, John Medlin, and Bernie Federly, facing page (left to right), for his success.

A Material World

A contemporary fuel Funny Car is a veritable collage of natural and man-made materials, the crucial properties of these materials being strength and light weight. Although the full inventory runs to about fifty different materials, the bulk is composed of aluminum alloys (engine block, rods, pistons, heads), alloy steels (frame, crankshaft, rear end), a four-element carbon-fiber graphite weave (the body), magnesium (spoiler), and Lexan™ (windows). In smaller quantities there are, on the mundane side, babbitt, brass, bronze, cadmium, cork, cotton, leather, nickel, nylon, paper, porcelain, rubber, silicon, vinyl, and zinc. On the exotic side are vulcanite, Stellite™, silver, and even a trace of gold!

From the '80s Funny Cars of *Jungle Jim Liberman, below, and Raymond Beadle, right, to modern machines like Chuck Etchells's Camaro driven by Whit Bazemore, opposite, technical advances have run speed records up right alongside those of the dragsters.*

DICK AND KIM LaHAIE

From the 1960s, Dick LaHaie had proven himself to be a superbly resourceful "privateer"—the term for a racer with no major sponsorship—and everyone knew that he'd be unbeatable with serious financial backing. That finally came about in 1987, and Dick promptly won the Top Fuel championship. Often at his side was his son, Jeff, but invariably there was his daughter, Kim, who had assumed the position of crew chief while still in her mid-twenties. Kim had always been curious about technical things, about mechanics, just like her dad and her brother. "What I do seems unusual to a lot of people," she remarked, "but, to me, it's just something that comes naturally."

Dick hung up his firesuit in the early '90s, then went on to a stellar career as a crew chief for a succession of Top Fuel operations, including two championship seasons with Scott Kalitta in 1994–95.

Kim put in a little seat time herself, then joined her husband, Tim Richards, as co-crew chiefs for Chuck Etchells. And what a pair!

Kim had her world championship with her father; Tim had five of his own as crew chief for Joe Amato. In eight years with Etchells, they finished lower than fifth in the standings only once, and in October 1993 Etchells had the first four-second run in a Funny Car, 4.98 at Topeka. Since then, they've apportioned the workload well, with Tim analyzing computer data, and Kim focusing on the maze of components that comprise the clutch-management system.

Kim LaHaie Richards worked on her dad's dragster as a teenager, then became an accomplished crew chief in her own right.

Dick LaHaie's renown as a driver/tuner led not only to a "second season" for himself as crew chief of today's Miller Lite Top Fueler, but also to a successful tuning career for his daughter, Kim.

Aerodynamic Finesse

"I started wondering why, as drag racers, we were racing cars that were a hundred miles per hour faster than Formula 1, yet our aerodynamic efforts were mired somewhere between that of a freight train and a tumbleweed." So said Henry Walther, a man with a lifetime of experience with fuel cars. There have been many streamlined dragsters over the years, from Jocko Johnson's full envelope of 1959 to Don Garlits' Swamp Rat 30 of 1986. Some were gorgeous. But none of them worked as intended and none of the top competitors to date has any streamlining device that stands out any more visibly than the flares in front of the rear tires.

With dragsters, it seems that multiplying horsepower is all that's required to go quicker and faster.

A Funny Car, on the other hand, has a myriad of aerodynamic subtleties, around the wheel wells and skirts, the hood scoop, the roof line, and many other places. Look closely and you will find contours that have been tweaked almost everywhere. This aerodynamic finesse has a lot to do with Funny Cars being just about as fast as Top Fuelers in spite of a considerable handicap in terms of weight.

hile most dragsters today still leave the wheels exposed, Leland Kolb, left, drove a car in the early 1970s that was streamlined to also gain downforce on the rear wheels for traction. Del Worsham's Funny Car, top, shows the sleek aerodynamics of twenty-first-century flopper designs.

JOE AMATO

Joe Amato began racing alcohol dragsters in the Winston Drag Racing Series, later known as Federal-Mogul. He garnered three victories there before moving to Top Fuel dragsters in 1982, where he became the first driver ever to win five NHRA Winston Top Fuel championships. He earned more Top Fuel wins—fifty-two in ninety-seven finals—than any driver in NHRA history, and never finished out of the top ten in the Winston standings.

Joe has always been a successful businessman, both inside drag racing and out. He started working full time at the age of sixteen after his father suffered a heart attack, and his Keystone Automotive Warehouse in Exeter, Pennsylvania, became the largest auto parts chain on the East Coast. With both sponsorship backing and his own money to support his drag racing operation, Joe and his team were able to spend time on research and development aimed at keeping their car among the fastest in the sport.

In 1984 Joe and his crew chief, Tim Richards, debuted a new setup—a wing cantilevered out behind the plane of the rear tires and seven feet high, out of the turbulence and up on "clean air." Amato went on to win the NHRA Winston Top Fuel championship that year—his first title. Racers called his innovation the "Kareem Abdul" wing. Within three years, speeds jumped from the 250s to the 280s, with Amato being first to pass the 260 mph mark and, later, 280 mph.

Early in the 2000 season, Joe suffered a tear in the retina of his right eye, probably due to the G-forces exerted on a driver when the chutes deploy at over 300 mph. Within six weeks of laser surgery he was racing again, this time with a chute that allows some of the air out to cushion the force with which the car is stopped. Joe retired as a driver at the end of the 2000 season.

The cantilevered wing pioneered by Joe Amato in 1984 is commonplace on modern Top Fuel dragsters.

Anatomy of a 21st-Century Funny Car

NHRA permits a 25-inch range in the wheelbase, from 100 to 125. Bodies are supposed to resemble cars less than five years old, and when in place, the front overhang must not exceed 40 inches. The spoiler cannot be more than 54 inches wide. These are serious restrictions, and yet today's Funny Cars are about as close as drag racing has ever come to all-out streamliners.

Mechanically, they aren't much different from Top Fuelers except for the oil pan, the blower drive, and the headers. A bare Funny Car chassis consists of about 180 feet (eighteen pieces) of tubing and weighs 125 pounds. Overall, with driver but without fuel, a Funny Car must weigh 2,325 pounds, 225 pounds heavier than a Top Fueler. This is why Funny Cars have four-wheel brakes, unlike dragsters. It also accounts for the ET records in the two classes usually being from two-tenths to three-tenths apart. The adage that "a hundred pounds is worth a tenth" seems to hold true today. Imagine how a Funny Car would perform if it weren't toting that $15,000, 250-pound body shell.

Cockpit safety cage

Dual parachutes

Wheelie bar

36" x 17" x 16" slicks

4130 chrome-moly steel chassis, 125" wheelbase

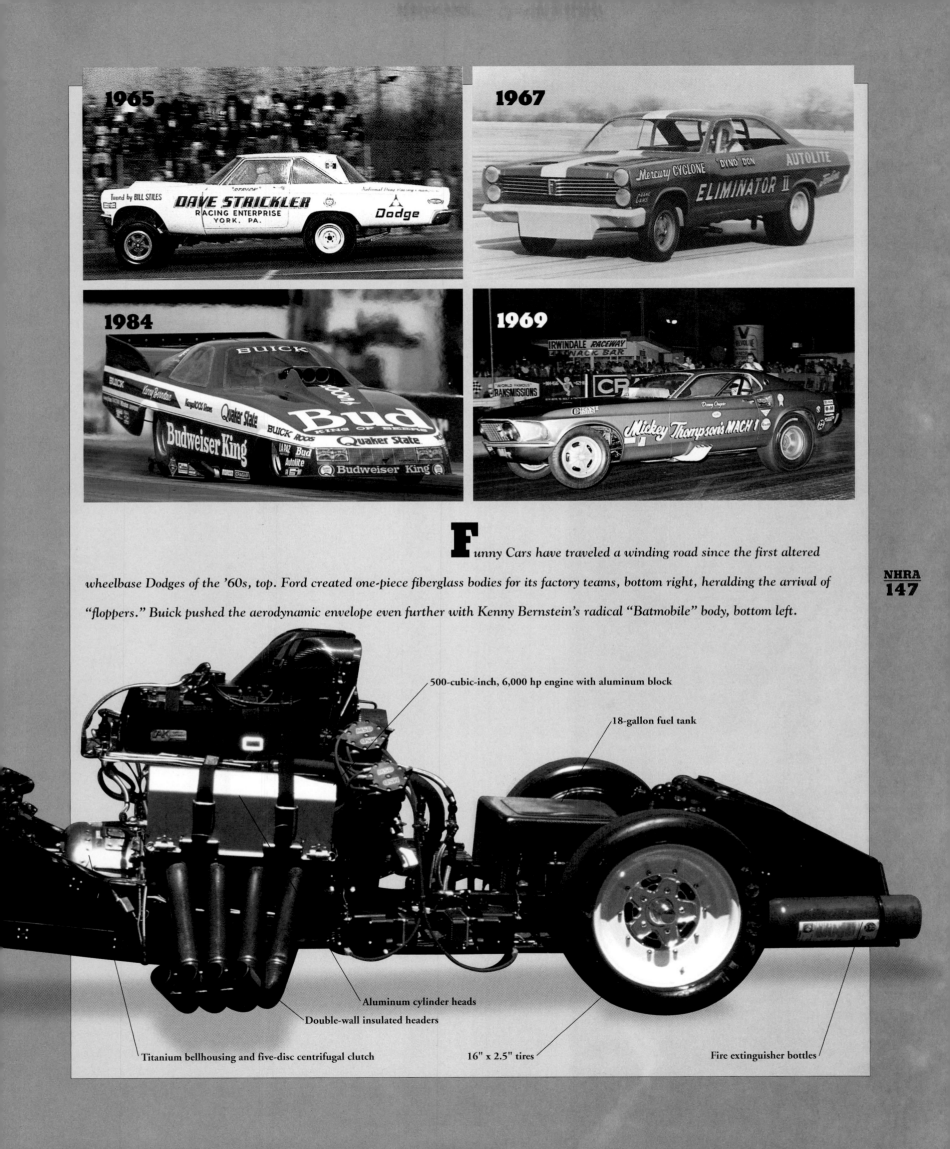

1965

DAVE STRICKLER
RACING ENTERPRISE
YORK, PA.

Dodge

1967

Mercury CYCLONE DYNO DON AUTOLITE

ELIMINATOR II

1984

BUICK

Bud
KING OF BEERS

Budweiser King

Quaker State

1969

IRWINDALE RACEWAY

Mickey Thompson's MACH I

Funny Cars have traveled a winding road since the first altered wheelbase Dodges of the '60s, top. Ford created one-piece fiberglass bodies for its factory teams, bottom right, heralding the arrival of "floppers." Buick pushed the aerodynamic envelope even further with Kenny Bernstein's radical "Batmobile" body, bottom left.

500-cubic-inch, 6,000 hp engine with aluminum block

18-gallon fuel tank

Aluminum cylinder heads

Double-wall insulated headers

Titanium bellhousing and five-disc centrifugal clutch

16" x 2.5" tires

Fire extinguisher bottles

ow the owner of an air-freight business, Connie Kalitta is equally at home flying an airplane or piloting a Top Fuel dragster.

CONNIE AND SCOTT KALITTA . . . AND NOW DOUG TOO

Ypsilanti, Michigan's, Conrad Kalitta first made a name in 1960 with a dragster called the Bounty Hunter, on the side of which he tallied his victories in shootouts against the top guns of the day. Then he pioneered with the single-overhead-cam Ford as a fuel engine, began winning events like the Winternationals, and kept winning even when he switched back to Chryslers. He captured a world championship with Shirley Muldowney in 1977, and their saga was dramatized in the movie *Heart Like a Wheel*. The closest he came to winning it on his own was third place in 1984 and again in 1985.

Around this same time, Connie and his son Scott began fielding a two-car team, and soon Scott was emerging as a force. Then he hooked up with Dick LaHaie, likewise just starting out as a "hired gun" crew chief after retiring from the cockpit. In 1993, Scott finished second in the Top Fuel standings to Eddie Hill, and in 1994 and 1995 he won handily over Don Prudhomme and Cory McClenathan. After 1996, when Scott finished second to Kenny Bernstein, his appearances on the championship trail became more sporadic, as were his dad's, largely because they were both consumed with the operation of Connie's huge air-freight business, American International Airways.

But NHRA fuel racing would not be NHRA fuel racing if a Kalitta were not in the thick of things, and soon enough another Kalitta emerged on the scene, driving under American International sponsorship. This was Doug Kalitta, Scott's cousin and Connie's nephew, who had worked as a crewman for Connie in the '80s. Later, Doug had made his own mark on oval tracks, as a winner in midgets and sprint cars and as the 1994 United States Auto Club sprint-car champion.

Although Doug had driven only roundy-round machinery, he took to Top Fuelers like a duck to water, finishing sixth in his first season and fifth in the next, with Uncle Connie handling the crew chief duties himself. With a bounteous sponsorship deal from the billion-dollar MGM Grand Hotel and Casino in Las Vegas in 2000, and with his uncle's experience, there was not much doubt about Doug improving considerably on those finishes.

Doug Kalitta, bottom, switched from sprint cars to Top Fuel racing. Cousin Scott, top, cut his teeth on the drag strips with Connie.

SHIRLEY MULDOWNEY

When Shirley Muldowney applied for her NHRA Top Fuel license in 1973 after a stint in Funny Cars, Don Garlits was one of the two drivers who signed the form attesting to her ability. The other was Connie Kalitta. Together, she and Kalitta won a world championship in 1977. After their breakup they became fiery rivals, but never was there a rivalry as impassioned as the one between Shirley and Garlits. Shirley, in her own words, had a "kick-ass attitude" as fierce as anyone's, and with Big Daddy she always gave as good as she got.

She won her second NHRA title in 1980, this time with Rahn Tobler as crew chief. No one had ever won two NHRA Top Fuel titles before. Shirley won three Top Fuel championships all told, as many as

Garlits won. Only Joe Amato won more. All three of her championships came before her brush with death in the aftermath of a 247 mph crash in Quebec in the summer of 1984. Eighteen months later, she hobbled over to her new Top Fueler and climbed in, and when news reporters asked why she had come back, she answered, "It's what I do."

With husband Rahn Tobler as crew chief, Shirley finished in NHRA's top ten five more times before shifting her focus to match racing, where she became the top draw. After Shirley paved the way, many other women obtained licenses to drive Top Fuelers, but so far none has ever approached her mastery or her record of conquests.

During the '70s and '80s, three-time Top Fuel champion Shirley Muldowney was a familiar face in the NHRA finals rounds. She returned to NHRA racing in 2000 at the Nationals in Indianapolis.

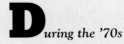

FAMILY

NHRA drag racing differs from other motorsports in so many ways, not least being its degree of family participation at all levels. One of the first and most fabled in the pro ranks was Don and Pat Garlits, who, with daughters Donna and Gay Lynn, seemed to travel everywhere together during the 1960s, '70s, and '80s (this is why Don was first dubbed "Daddy"). One of the most popular Top Fuel teams from the same period was Jim and Alison Lee, and who can forget Tom Hoover with his Ma and Pa, Ruth and George? In the '90s no couple was more beloved than Eddie and Ercie Hill.

Today, there are the likes of Warren, Arlene, and Kurt Johnson in Pro Stock and Jim and Diane Dunn in fuel Funny Car. There is a long series of crew chief partnerships, from the Lees to Tim and Kim Richards, Kim being the daughter of all-time great driver and tuner Dick LaHaie. Kim has had her time in the cockpit as well, and the list of female fuel dragster drivers just goes on and on, many with dads or boyfriends or husbands turning the wrenches. Far and away the best known, of course, is Shirley Muldowney and husband Rahn Tobler, but one should not forget Shelly Anderson and her dad, Brad. Or Danielle DePorter, Lori Johns, or Lucille Lee, all top ten finishers over the years.

With the second generation° in NHRA, the examples are too numerous to include all of them here. So many of today's stars have grown up in the sport—Tony Schumacher, Larry Dixon Jr., Mike Dunn, Scott Kalitta, Shelly and Randy Anderson, Doug Herbert, Del Worsham, Pat Austin, all the Coughlins and Pedregons—not to mention the stars-in-waiting like Melanie Troxel, Ronda Hartman-Smith, and Andrew Cowin.

Drag racing has long been a family affair, with husbands and wives sharing the load. Jim and Alison Lee, facing page, campaigned a Top Fuel dragster in the '70s, and Eddie and Ercie Hill, top, won a championship together in 1993. Like many sportsman teams, the Richardsons, left, race as a family unit.

unny Car pilots Frank, Cruz, and Tony Pedregon,

left to right, have kept alive the memory of their legendary father, "Flamin' Frank" Pedregon.

Larry Dixon Sr. holds young Larry Jr. even

more carefully than his trophy as they both celebrate Dad's Top Fuel dragster victory in the 1970

Winternationals. Larry Jr. never ventured far from the pits he obviously relished even back then,

growing up to drive a Top Fuel dragster for owner Don Prudhomme and crew chief Dick LaHaie.

WARREN, ARLENE, AND KURT JOHNSON

Bob and Etta Glidden. Jim and Alison Lee. Eddie and Ercie Hill. Since the beginning, drag racing has always had its first families. Presently, many fans would agree that the reigning first family is the Johnsons of Buford, Georgia. The patriarch is Warren, "the Professor of Pro Stock" who dominated drag racing's most demanding class in the 1990s, a man whose accomplishments would fill volumes: eighty-one national event victories, over 120 top qualifying spots and low

elapsed-time marks, over 180 top-speed-of-the-event marks and 700 round wins, thirteen years without a DNQ, five NHRA championships, and eight runner-ups. The list can go on forever.

But Warren Johnson will be the first to tell you how essential his wife, Arlene, has been to all of this. Today, Arlene is the team's business manager, her responsibilities including everything from making travel arrangements to videotaping every run down the track. But they both remember the lean times before they moved from Minnesota to Georgia, when they slept in their truck and showered "in our friends' hotel rooms at the races." And there was the family dog, too, and there

was Kurt. Warren and Arlene started going to the races together in 1961, and when WJ turned pro in 1975—2000 was his silver anniversary—Kurt was twelve. Getting to come along, his parents insisted, was conditional on keeping an "A" average in school; not once did Kurt miss a race. In those days, he also swept the shop; today, having worked in his dad's shop for eighteen years, he is the engine builder, responsible for all machine work, assembly, and testing. And, oh, yes, Kurt Johnson has a

pretty successful racing operation of his own.

Kurt's rookie year was 1993. He won on the national event circuit three times and finished second in the points standings—second to his dad. In the years since, he has finished fifth, third, fourth, and then third three times in a row, even as his dad was finishing third, first, second twice, and first twice. Talk about a pair of heavy hitters! Says Kurt, "Dad and I have the same parts, and we should be as quick on the track. If we both do our jobs, we should meet in the final round on race day."

They have met a few times, and KJ is holding his own. After only seven years of full-time driving, he has nineteen career victories and stands fourth among active Pro Stock shoes. That still leaves him short of his dad's total, but Kurt is quite aware that his dad didn't get his first victory until he was

thirty-nine, older than Kurt is now. And it was Kurt, not his dad, who was first to put a Pro Stocker in the sixes, a 6.98 at Englishtown on May 20, 1994. "I'll never learn everything Dad knows," Kurt remarks, "but I'm going to try."

As for Mom, she still remembers back to before Kurt was born, when racing was purely a hobby. Lots of former weekend warriors will tell you that they didn't expect to be where they are today. Surely, Arlene Johnson could never have dreamed of 26,000 square feet of

shop space, a whole lineup of race cars, enduring support from General Motors. She couldn't have imagined their universally envied research and development program set up to approach the sport of drag racing as a science back in the days when she was cradling Kurt in her arms while Warren drove their C/Modified Production '57 Chevy to one or another obscure drag strip on the northern plains, their fondest hope being to return home with a nice trophy.

Warren and Arlene Johnson, top, began racing together in 1961. Son Kurt, bottom, joined them in 1993, showing the same tenacity as his five-time Winston champion father in the pursuit of Pro Stock excellence.

Jr. Drag Racing League

And then there are the real youngsters. For kids as young as eight, NHRA sponsors the Jr. Drag Racing League. Jr. Dragsters are half-scale models of rear-engine fuelers, designed and fabricated the same way, and equipped with single-cylinder 5 hp Briggs and Stratton engines. They race for half the conventional distance, for 660 feet not 1,320, under either of two formats: one patterned on NHRA's ET brackets with a dial-your-own handicap, the other heads-up with a set breakout, as with Super Comp and Super Gas. There are eight different age brackets. Competitors ten and older are permitted to go as quick as

8.90 in the eighth mile without breaking out; eight-and nine-year-olds can go 12.90. The rules allow a wide variety of engine modifications, with either gasoline or alcohol as fuel, so the Jr. Dragsters serve as a school for tuners as well as for drivers.

Youngsters competing at NHRA member tracks nationwide amass points toward qualifying for the National Championships, held under the same rules and format as

NHRA's "regular" championship series. Even though the Jr. Drag Racing League is relatively new—it began in 1992—competitors who cut their teeth there have already started moving up into the ranks of NHRA's ET bracket and Sportsman classes, and one of them, Richie Stevens, has emerged as a top competitor in Pro Stock. It is just a matter of time before others begin graduating into the professional ranks, and emerging as winners—having begun to master drag racing's fine points long before they could qualify for a state learner's permit!

The Jr. Drag Racing League, introduced by NHRA in 1992, has

been responsible not only for cultivating young drivers, but also for cultivating family relationships as fathers, sons, mothers, and daughters

learn to work together as competitive race teams.

JIM, TONI, JAMIE, JOHN, AND MELISSA YATES

"The key to being successful in life is finding something you love and doing it with a passion," says Jim Yates. Jim's first passion is his family, his wife Toni and his three children. Then, there is the chain of auto-parts stores in the Washington, D.C., area that he operates along with Toni. Oh, and then there are Pro Stockers, in which he finished no worse than fourth in the standings in the 1990s and won two consecutive championships in 1996 and 1997.

Racing has always been a family affair for the Yateses. Toni

has been an active partner since Jim's days as a bracketeer at Maryland International in Budds Creek. They went to the University of Maryland together, Jim studying mechanical engineering and Toni graphic arts. Today Toni is team manager, as well as having mechanical responsibilities with the engines; son Jamie, an engineering student at Maryland, is in charge of the transmission, clutch, and computer, as well as being a sometime driver; and son John, just entering college, takes care of the drivetrain and tires. Daughter Melissa, a student at Clemson University, is the family's "head cheerleader."

The proof of this combination is in the results: fifth all-time in Pro Stock victories.

A *fast family: Second-generation driver Jamie, left, hopes to carry on the Yates tradition of winning Pro Stock championships under the watchful eyes of his parents, Jim and Toni, facing page.*

The Shootout

You're in the cockpit of a Funny Car, wrapped in a Nomex cocoon so tight that you couldn't scratch an itch if you tried. You rationalize that this space-age jumpsuit may save your life if your engine kicks the rods out and burning oil and nitro torch your car's fiberglass shell. You try to relax as the attendants go through the complicated ritual of cinching, fastening, and tightening belts, straps, and harnesses.

Voices spew from the speakers and it is all gibberish to you. You hear your name and this gets your attention for a moment, but then you tune it out and try to concentrate on what comes next. Other sensations creep into your consciousness. You haven't eaten all day. You're feeling like a caged beast. No—you're a gunfighter, a desperado, with

more notches in your pistol than the leading men in all of John Ford's classic westerns. And it seems that every punk with a firesuit comes gunning for you.

You hear your name over the public address again and then the name of the guy in the other lane. Your heart speeds up for a moment, but you concentrate more clearly now. This so-called shootout between you and the other driver is a fabrication. This isn't a contest of wills, you tell yourself, not just driver against driver, or driver against machine—this is a battle that pits you against yourself.

But it isn't that simple, either. You're not in a vacuum. There are reputations. Your team's. Your sponsor's. Your own. Beneath all that, you just want to survive. And you want the win lights in your lane.

As a track worker sprays torrents of water into the burnout box, one of your crew chiefs leans into the cockpit and says that the track has cooled down and doesn't have as much traction as it did earlier. You make out some of what he says, but mostly you are mesmerized by the blackened, frayed end of the toothpick bobbing at the corner of his mouth with every word.

You try to wipe this conversation from your consciousness as a crew member pours a beaker of alcohol into the fuel tank. This dilutes the nitro mixture to about 88 percent, a strategic move to calm down your brutal machine and enable it to make traction on a surface that is suddenly slippery and cold. The beaker tells you that now everything else is wrong: the clutch timers, the spark advance, the overdriven speed of the supercharger.

The starter does a pirouette, spins both forefingers in the air, and shouts, "Fire in the hole!" Your crew chief points at you and you stare at that toothpick while another crew member clicks the switch on an aircraft starter motor that suddenly whirrs to life. Your crew chief yanks a wire off the magneto that was grounding out any spark. At ignition, he lowers the lid on the carbon-fiber shell that passes for the body of a Funny Car.

The lights dim and the sound around you mutes. It is surprisingly quiet in this setting as the greater part of the cackle and thunder remains outside the confines of your environment. This is the eye of the hurricane.

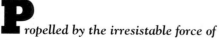

Propelled by the irresistible force of 12,000 hp, Kenny Bernstein and Gary Scelzi hurtle toward the finish line in a classic Top Fuel duel.

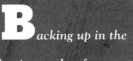

Backing up in the hot, sticky tire tracks after a burnout is no easy feat when you're trapped inside the claustrophobic confines of a Funny Car.

T om Hoover, foreground, had a competitive fire that burned long and hot. He began racing Top Fuel dragsters in 1964, was one of the first drivers to switch from top fuelers to Funny Cars, and continued racing them into the 1990s.

Chief starter Rick Stewart is the man in the middle, the final authority who oversees the staging process, gives the drivers a final safety check, and then sends them racing toward the finish line with a flick of his finger when he triggers the Christmas Tree.

After you roll through the burnout box, you stomp on the loud pedal. An explosion of sound saturates the cockpit and your heart accelerates again. It is deafening to your own ears, but excruciating to those in the crosshairs of the exhaust. You hammer it to 5,000 rpm and smoke from burning rubber envelops the starting line. As you stop the car about 300 feet down the track you can sense an entire stadium on its feet, cheering with such ferocity that its roar creeps over the tone of the engine.

Then you hear the sound of another car on your left, tire smoke billowing. The other driver is literally stealing your thunder, and by leaving after you and taking his burnout further, has chosen to let you look at him through the undulating haze the entire time you're reversing back toward the starting line.

Your car's body is raised for a few seconds and the guy with the ever-present toothpick turns on the second magneto, a move that doubles the amperage to the spark plugs.

The body is lowered and the toothpick motions you toward the starting beams. Two feet away from blastoff, the toothpick reaches onto the engine's protruding injector hat and pulls away a piece of tape that reminds him to remove the throttle stop. This limiter in the throttle linkage prevents you from blowing the thing up on the burnout in case you get a little excited. Another crew member walks into your vision with a red flag emblazoned with the words "REMOVE BEFORE FLIGHT." This means that the cotter pin has been removed from the parachute packs and that, yes, they will actually open when you hit the lever at 320 mph.

You engage the first beam of the Christmas Tree and reach for the switch that will double the volume of nitro pouring into the combustion chambers. With the engine's potential for detonation doubled, its tone is now much lower, and ironically, softer in

It's the thrill of the battle that lures even the most war-torn drag racers back to the starting line week after week, round after round, no matter what the financial, emotional, or physical cost.

volume. The low tones throb like a mantra and you are in a transcendental state, answering only to the commands of an inner voice that has guided you down the drag strip thousands of times before. If somebody drove an ice pick into the skin between your fingers you wouldn't flinch. You are a fire walker.

Not that the other guy isn't trying to disturb your focus. He rotates a wheel and goes in deep, staging the car so far into the beams that he has turned off the top bulb, mere inches from a false start. He's doing this in the hope that the flickering bulbs are enough to jar your focus. It doesn't work.

> ## "I feel like a warrior when I get in the car."
> —FUNNY CAR DRIVER RON CAPPS

The light flashes green and you can hear only your own engine, roaring at 8,000 rpm. This is good. It means you're out on the other guy. You feel a hand pushing into your chest at five Gs, and suddenly the sound around you changes, which is not good. The pitch of your motor blips higher, and there's a low rumble on your periphery. This means you are losing traction and spinning the tires, and the other car is right next to you. Worse, you catch a glimpse of his front wheels. *If I can see him, it means I'm losing,* you tell yourself.

Despite the G-forces, you feather the throttle and try to ignore the wheel in the corner of your eye. But curiosity gets the best of you. You look over at the car beside you and have the eerie feeling you're both standing still. Your opponent has also overpowered the track. You stand on the throttle and the motor roars in defiance.

The cold track can't handle the horsepower. Again you pedal the accelerator and again your nemesis roars by. In a flash you recognize that the guy in the other lane isn't the thorn in your paw, it's this throttle that sends your tires spinning in vain.

Again, he strikes the tires, and so it goes. You stand on the throttle again in a motion whose impulses confuse the timers on the clutch management system and the programmable magneto retards. In the chaos, the tachometer needle goes into orbit and the fuel pumps respond by flooding the cylinders with raw nitro. You know if you whap the throttle one time too many the puddled fuel will detonate and the crankshaft will snap and carve a window in the block, all of which could send molten geysers of burning oil and fuel onto the car's body.

But this time you cheat the hangman. No boom. No fire. Just a win light. You hit the chutes, the brakes, and the fuel shut-off switch and coast across the shutdown area, the motor dieseling just a little bit. Luckily, the guy in the other lane gave up after he smoked the baloneys a third time.

Steam and smoke smolder off the engine as the safety crew raises the lid, and someone puts a microphone in your face and wants to know how it feels to win yet again, and how close you came to disaster. You feel queasy from the hunger and the smoke you've inhaled, and all you can think of to say is, "This is a helluva of a way to make a living." And so it is.

s drag racing's worldwide popularity grew

throughout the decades, high-dollar racing facilities dubbed "supertracks" began to dot the NHRA

landscape. Upon its debut in 2000, The Strip at Las Vegas Motor Speedway instantly became the

facility against which all other supertracks would be measured.

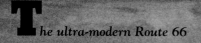**T**he ultra-modern Route 66

Raceway near Chicago, Illinois, opened in 1999. Seventy-five

thousand drag racing fans can watch the drama of side-by-side racing

NHRA style.

The Shutdown

This is a place familiar to fans from seeing it on television, but usually out of their sight when at the races. It's almost the reverse image of the staging area, the place where every run comes to an end (unless, of course, something dire happened along the way). First-time visitors to the shutdown are always struck by the sounds of a car decelerating, whether it be a dragster or door car. The swoosh of massive tires, the whistle of a fully inflated parachute, and frequently, by the end of the run, the rattle of one thing or another. By the time a driver is about to turn off the engine, the parachute is dragging on the ground, a final shuffling sound at the quiet end of another furious run.

Guided by a track worker stationed at a turnoff, the driver swings a lazy arc, and as soon as the car is off the course, where things aren't so smooth, it usually rattles plenty.

Unbuckling and climbing out of the seat takes a few seconds (a few more if a Funny Car pilot has to climb out the roof hatch); stripping off firesuit, boots, gloves, helmet, collar, and

headsock takes longer. After making sure everything is okay, track workers return their attention to the track and the next pair coming down. So, after throwing the parachute over the wing or spoiler, the driver may often have a minute or two to collect some thoughts alone, even if the other driver happens to have pulled up nearby.

A push vehicle may approach in any number of ways, depending on the outcome of the run. A strong qualifying number, a round win, and the horn may be honking and the crew members leaning out, waving and shouting. A final-round win, and the approach may be bedlam, followed by embraces and sometimes even tears, as television crews gather nearby. But the scene can be quite different if it is the last round of qualifying and the car was left on the wrong side of the bump. Then, the approach may be slow, even grim. Or, if the driver feels let down by the crew chief, or vice versa, there may even be harsh words. If the stakes are high, somebody may even get fired, at least temporarily.

In drag racing's early days, a winning driver entered the shutdown area with little fanfare, save for the Safety Safari. Today when the winning car rolls to a stop at the far end, the driver may celebrate with a contingent of photographers, sponsors, and interviewers.

Whether they're joyous or disconsolate, the crew still has to gather things together and hitch up the towing strap. Then somebody climbs into the cockpit—maybe the driver, maybe not—and the little procession heads back toward the pits. Inside the tow vehicle, silence may reign, but usually the air is filled with a babble of voices. What went right?

What went wrong? If things did go wrong, the recriminations may fade before the team arrives back in the pits. If not, they usually fade soon after. Every drag racer knows that, in this sport, where fractions of a second separate winners from the rest, sometimes you eat the bear, and sometimes the bear eats you.

Tony Schumacher, left, enjoys the jubilation and relief of victory at the end of a long weekend.

The shutdown area can be dangerous. Though no longer running at top speed, a race car that has rounded the turnoff, parachutes still billowing behind it, can't be taken lightly.

In 1996 a popular young Top Fuel driver named Blaine Johnson seemed destined for stardom. Racing with his brother Alan as owner and crew chief, Blaine was almost a shoo-in for the NHRA Winston Top Fuel championship when he died in a tragic crash during a qualifying run at the U. S. Nationals at Indianapolis.

The Alan Johnson team quit racing for the season, but Blaine had such a large points lead that he almost won the title posthumously. When Kenny Bernstein won it, he gave Alan Johnson the trophy. It wasn't the way Alan wanted to win.

In a spectacular tribute to the memory of the fallen Blaine Johnson, Team Winston, left, led by (left to right), Blaine's brother Alan, father, Everett, and Gary Scelzi, won the 1997 Top Fuel championship with Rookie of the Year driver Scelzi, top, at the wheel.

GARY

The next season the Johnson racing team was back again, with another young driver—a rookie named Gary Scelzi. Scelzi was not a newcomer to dragster driving, having won six Top Alcohol Dragster division event victories in 1995 and 1996. And Gary Scelzi didn't drive like a rookie Top Fueler. In fact, he took the class by storm in 1997, becoming the first rookie to win the NHRA Winston Top Fuel championship, and to prove he was no fluke, he repeated as champion in 1998.

In 1999 he finished a close second to Tony Schumacher, and though it was disappointing not to defend his championship, Scelzi became the first NHRA driver ever to record two passes below 4.500 seconds. Alan Johnson Racing's record of success in the 1990s continued in 2000 when they won the championship. Teamed with their determined star driver Gary Scelzi and buttressed by the memory of Blaine Johnson, they're a force to be reckoned with for years to come.

With Blaine, bottom and bottom right, at the wheel, and Alan turning the wrenches, Johnson Family Racing was "the race team that could" in 1996, well on their way to the Top Fuel championship when Blaine's life was cut short by a qualifying crash at the U.S. Nationals.

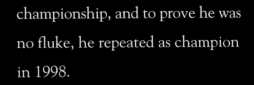

Nearly a half-century

of NHRA racing did not dull the competitive fire

evident in the eyes of Chris Karamesines.

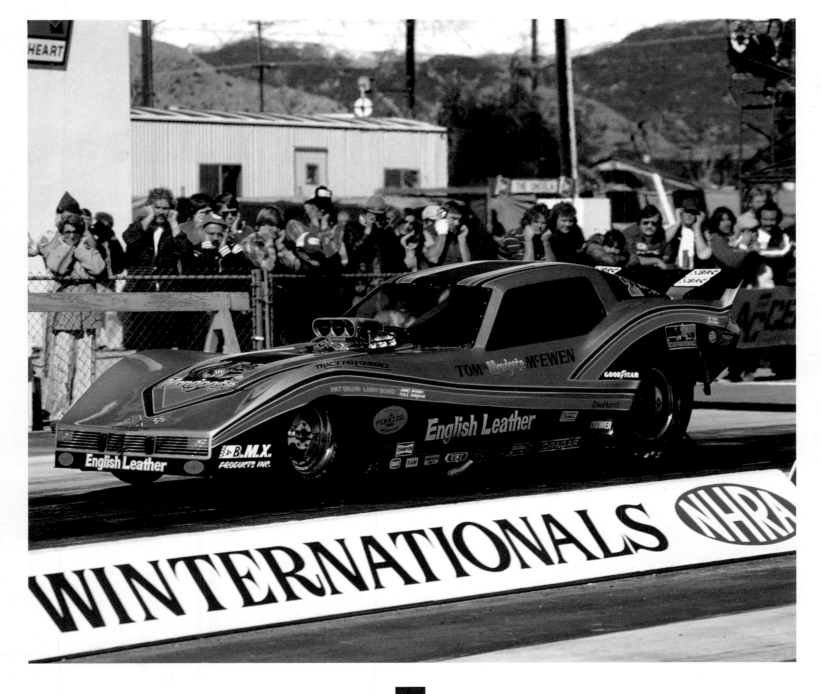

Tom "Mongoose" McEwen was the perfect foil for

his partner Don "Snake" Prudhomme. McEwen the businessman and Prudhomme the racer were an

odd couple who became household names. McEwen was one of the few Funny Car drivers who found

success in a Corvette; he began and ended his remarkable career in dragsters.

1971

With a drag racing career that's spanned more than fifty years, Jim Dunn has been in and out of more cars than a driving school teacher. In fact, he started drag racing just after getting his driver's license at age sixteen on Ball Road in Anaheim in the early '50s. He has raced everything from a Fiat-bodied altered to Top Fuel dragsters and Funny Cars.

By the 1960s, Jim had moved from the Fiat altered to slingshot dragsters, winning Bakersfield in 1969 with the Rainbow Car. Within a few years, however, the slingshot design was blown out of contention by rear-engine fuelers, and Jim had moved on to Funny Cars. Having seen the effectiveness of the rear-engine design in dragsters, the Dunn Reath team experimented with the same setup in a Funny Car. They incorporated the air scoop into the roof, but that design wasn't allowed. The first car, with the driver moved forward and the motor lowered, just didn't handle

right, so they went back to the drawing boards. Dunn's 1972 Barracuda was the only rear-engine Funny Car to win a national event—the 1972 Supernationals. It had no roof scoop. Air got to the engine through two holes in the windshield, with tubes funneling back to the supercharger.

Many cars and victories later, Jim Dunn became an owner, still in the quest for an elusive NHRA season championship in Funny Cars and solid proof that the competitive fires ignited half a century ago in the early days of the sport continued to burn brightly.

NHRA
183

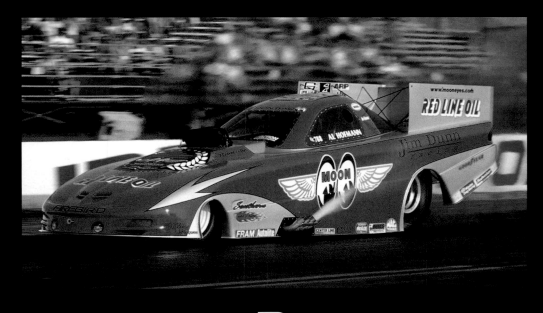

Big Jim Dunn does things his way, whether it's building a rear-engined Funny Car, facing page and top, or running his own front-engine Funny Car racing team, bottom.

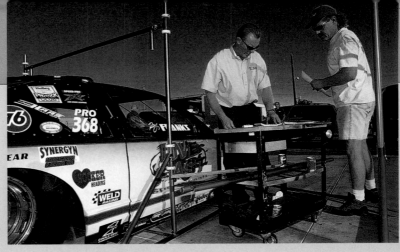

A Choice for Everyone

Through an ingenious array of options tailored to individual preferences and pocketbooks, the National Hot Rod Association sanctions competition under more than 220 classifications at three primary levels. At the professional level, the classes include Top Fuel dragsters, fuel Funny Cars, Pro Stocks, Pro Stock Trucks, and Pro Stock Motorcycles. This is drag racing's "big show," presented under RJR/Winston sponsorship in a spectacular tournament comprising twenty-two national events scheduled throughout the year.

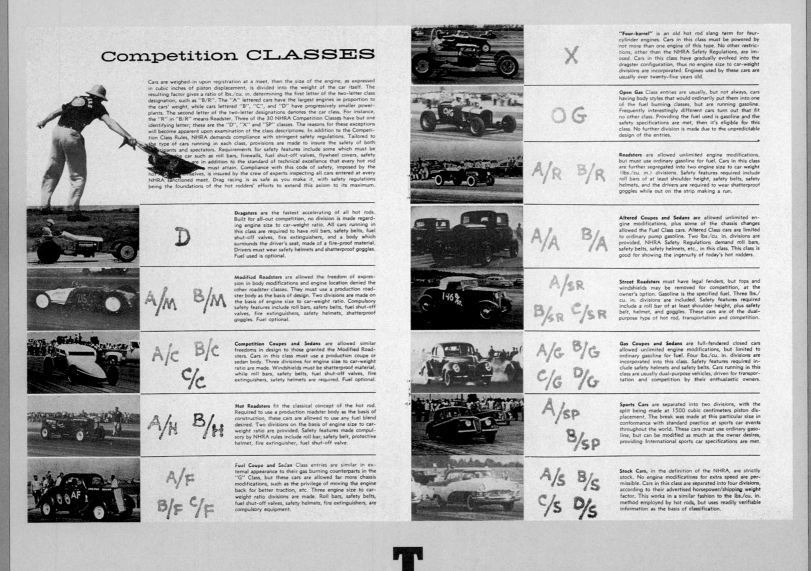

Competition CLASSES

Cars are weighed-in upon registration at a meet, then the size of the engine, as expressed in cubic inches of piston displacement, is divided into the weight of the car itself. The resulting factor gives a ratio of lbs./cu. in. determining the first letter of the two-letter class designation, such as "B/R". The "A" lettered cars have the largest engines in proportion to the cars' weight, while cars lettered "B", "C", and "D" have progressively smaller power-plants. The second letter of the two-letter designations denotes the car class. For instance, the "R" in "B/R" means Roadster. Three of the 30 NHRA Competition Classes have but one identifying letter; these are the "D", "X" and "SP" classes. The reasons for these exceptions will become apparent upon examination of the class descriptions. In addition to the Competition Class Rules, NHRA demands compliance with stringent safety regulations. Tailored to the type of cars running in each class, provisions are made to insure the safety of both participants and spectators. Requirements for safety features include some which must be on the car such as roll bars, firewalls, fuel shut-off valves, flywheel covers, safety ... are in addition to the standard of technical excellence that every hot rod ... must attain. Compliance with this code of safety, imposed by the ... themselves, is insured by the crew of experts inspecting all cars entered at every NHRA sanctioned meet. Drag racing is as safe as you make it, with safety regulations being the foundations of the hot rodders' efforts to extend this axiom to its maximum.

D — Dragsters are the fastest accelerating of all hot rods. Built for all-out competition, no division is made regarding engine size to car-weight ratio. All cars running in this class are required to have roll bars, safety belts, fuel shut-off valves, fire extinguishers, and a body which surrounds the driver's seat, made of a fire-proof material. Drivers must wear safety helmets and shatterproof goggles. Fuel used is optional.

A/M B/M — Modified Roadsters are allowed the freedom of expression in body modifications and engine location denied the other roadster classes. They must use a production roadster body as the basis of design. Two divisions are made on the basis of engine size to car-weight ratio. Compulsory safety features include roll bars, safety belts, fuel shut-off valves, fire extinguishers, safety helmets, shatterproof goggles. Fuel optional.

A/C B/C C/C — Competition Coupes and Sedans are allowed similar freedoms in design to those granted the Modified Roadsters. Cars in this class must use a production coupe or sedan body. Three divisions for engine size to car-weight ratio are made. Windshields must be shatterproof material, while roll bars, safety belts, fuel shut-off valves, fire extinguishers, safety helmets are required. Fuel optional.

A/H B/H — Hot Roadsters fit the classical concept of the hot rod. Required to use a production roadster body as the basis of construction, these cars are allowed to use any fuel blend desired. Two divisions on the basis of engine size to car-weight ratio are provided. Safety features made compulsory by NHRA rules include roll bar, safety belt, protective helmet, fire extinguisher, fuel shut-off valve.

A/F B/F C/F — Fuel Coupe and Sedan Class entries are similar in external appearance to their gas burning counterparts in the "G" Class, but these cars are allowed far more chassis modifications, such as the privilege of moving the engine back for better traction, etc. Three engine size to car-weight ratio divisions are made. Roll bars, safety belts, fuel shut-off valves, safety helmets, fire extinguishers, are compulsory equipment.

X — "Four-barrel" is an old hot rod slang term for four-cylinder engines. Cars in this class must be powered by not more than one engine of this type. No other restrictions, other than the NHRA Safety Regulations, are imposed. Cars in this class have gradually evolved into the dragster configuration, thus no engine size to car-weight divisions are incorporated. Engines used by these cars are usually over twenty-five years old.

O/G — Open Gas Class entries are usually, but not always, cars having body styles that would ordinarily put them into one of the fuel burning classes, but are running gasoline. Frequently interestingly different cars turn out that fit no other class. Providing the fuel used is gasoline and the safety specifications are met, then it's eligible for this class. No further division is made due to the unpredictable design of the entries.

A/R B/R — Roadsters are allowed unlimited engine modifications, but must use ordinary gasoline for fuel. Cars in this class are further segregated into two engine size to car weight (lbs./cu. in.) divisions. Safety features required include roll bars of at least shoulder height, safety belts, safety helmets, and the drivers are required to wear shatterproof goggles while out on the strip making a run.

A/A B/A — Altered Coupes and Sedans are allowed unlimited engine modifications, plus some of the chassis changes allowed the Fuel Class cars. Altered Class cars are limited to ordinary pump gasoline. Two lbs./cu. in. divisions are provided. NHRA Safety Regulations demand roll bars, safety belts, safety helmets, etc., in this class. This class is good for showing the ingenuity of today's hot rodders.

A/SR B/SR C/SR — Street Roadsters must have legal fenders, but tops and windshields may be removed for competition, at the owner's option. Gasoline is the specified fuel. Three lbs./cu. in. divisions are included. Safety features required include a roll bar of at least shoulder height, plus safety belt, helmet, and goggles. These cars are of the dual-purpose type of hot rod, transportation and competition.

A/G B/G C/G D/G — Gas Coupes and Sedans are full-fendered closed cars allowed unlimited engine modifications, but limited to ordinary gasoline for fuel. Four lbs./cu. in. divisions are incorporated into this class. Safety features required include safety helmets and safety belts. Cars running in this class are usually dual-purpose vehicles, driven for transportation and competition by their enthusiastic owners.

A/SP B/SP — Sports Cars are separated into two divisions, with the split being made at 1500 cubic centimeters piston displacement. The break was made at this particular size in conformance with standard practice at sports car events throughout the world. These cars must use ordinary gasoline, but can be modified as much as the owner desires, providing International sports car specifications are met.

A/S B/S C/S D/S — Stock Cars, in the definition of the NHRA, are strictly stock. No engine modifications for extra speed are permissible. Cars in this class are separated into four divisions, according to their advertised horsepower/shipping weight factor. This works in a similar fashion to the lbs./cu. in. method employed by hot rods, but uses readily verifiable information as the basis of classification.

This page from the first NHRA Nationals at Kansas City in 1955 gives a taste of the variety of cars and racing classes in the sport. Many of these cars were the roots of today's Sportsman Class machines.

A Choice for Everyone:
The Sportsmen

Sportsman racers are the backbone of NHRA drag racing. NHRA has created a structure supported by a broad base of grassroots racers in NHRA Street Legal programs, NHRA Summit Racing Series, the Castrol GTX Jr. Drag Racing League, and local events at 144 NHRA member tracks.

With the Street Legal program, NHRA returned to its roots. Enthusiasts race the same cars they drive to work and school, just as drag racing's pioneers did. The Castrol GTX Jr. Drag Racing League pits youngsters from eight to seventeen in half-size dragsters, an introduction to drag racing that can

lead to lifelong involvement. In the Summit Racing Series, family sedans and dragsters compete on an equal footing. Alcohol Funny Cars and dragsters headline the Federal-Mogul Drag Racing Series for more than 36,000 licensed NHRA competitors, who gain valuable experience while also competing for substantial awards.

In the Federal-Mogul Racing Series, races between *Competition Eliminator cars often feature staggered starts. Here, the dragster of David Rampy, foreground, was matched against the Trans AM of Tony Affonti.*

NHRA Sportsman racing features every vehicle and engine mix: fours, sixes, eights, roadsters, and streamliners. The "Super" classes—Super Street, Super Gas, and Super Comp—feature the closest races on the planet. Once the domain of '60s, muscle cars, the Stock and Super Stock classes have been revitalized by new-generation GT cars and fuel-injected machines from Detroit.

In Competition Eliminator, classic hot rods, gas-burning dragsters, and aerodynamic coupes compete with a range of powerplants from air-cooled four-cylinder engines and inline sixes to supercharged V-8s. NHRA Sportsman racers are an army of weekend warriors who march to the beat of racing engines. They have helped to make NHRA the world's largest motorsports sanctioning body. While the professionals are in the spotlight at national events, it is the thousands of Sportsman racers who give NHRA drag racing its creativity, strength, vitality, and enduring spirit.

A Choice for Everyone:
Super Comp, Super Gas, and Super Street

Competitors in these classes run heads-up with a 0.5 Tree, like the Pros and Sportsmen, but there is also a breakout, as in the ET brackets: 8.90, 9.90, or 10.90. In Super Comp, one sees mostly dragsters; Super Gas is reserved for full-bodied cars with full fenders, many of which are roadsters; and Super Street is restricted to full-bodied, full-fendered cars, vans, and trucks. All three classes are popular with racers and fans alike, because of the great variety of machinery and also because of the particular finesse required of drivers: they must be quick enough to win, but not too quick. Racers must beat their opponents, of course, but they automatically lose if they run under that .90 breakout.

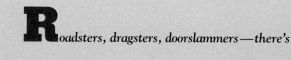

Roadsters, dragsters, doorslammers—there's *a place for every one of them in NHRA's Super categories.*

Over the years, the 8.90-second Super Comp category has become a haven for dragsters, although other vehicles are allowed. Cars crowd the staging lanes when the extremely popular class is called to run.

DARRELL GWYNN

He had it all before him, a young man in what was becoming an oldster's game: Don Garlits and Eddie Hill were thirty years older, Shirley Muldowney and Joe Amato twenty years. After a successful apprenticeship in alcohol machines (the way to the big show for many of today's fuel stars), Darrell Gwynn first made the Top Fuel rankings in 1985 in sixth place, then moved right up to second in 1986. After he nipped at Don Garlits's heels for the entire season, Garlits dubbed him "the Wolf" because he was so hungry. He finished no lower than fourth until 1989.

Then tragedy struck. Darrell was making an exhibition run near London, England, on Easter Sunday of 1990, when his chassis broke in two at more than 200 mph. In the horrific crash that followed, he lost his left arm and his spine was crushed at the fifth cervical vertebra. The grim reality of such a crush injury was inevitable paralysis.

Darrell Gwynn, right, with Wally Parks, center, and Mike Brotherton, a winner in dragsters, a champion in life after his accident.

But Darrell showed every bit as much courage as Muldowney had shown after her crash in Canada six years earlier. No, he never got back into the cockpit, but he became a familiar figure around the pits in his wheelchair, always confident, always smiling, and he redoubled his efforts to win the championship.

In 1992 he put Mike Brotherton in the cockpit and finished eighth. Then he made a deal with another second-generation racer like himself, Mike Dunn.

After that, Darrell Gwynn Racing was always in the hunt, and in 1999 Mike had the third-best winning percentage, won all of his four final rounds, and clocked the fourth-quickest ET in history, a 4.503. In 2000 Darrell and Mike found themselves without a sponsor, and temporarily absent from the NHRA championship chase. But nobody doubted that it would be only temporary, for Darrell Gwynn had already conquered much greater adversity than that.

Once the last refuge of the classic muscle cars of the '60s, Stock Eliminator was revitalized by a new generation of high-tech machines from Detroit. Stock Eliminator champion Al Corda has changed with the times, forsaking carburetors for computers when he switched to a fuel-injected Firebird.

Some say that an alcohol-burning Federal-Mogul Funny Car is the most difficult car to drive in drag racing. Think about shifting gears on a five-second pass and you'll understand why.

A Choice for Everyone: Dial Your Own

The Pro and Sportsman classes race under handicap starts. An image of two machines charging off together is what comes to mind for most people when they think of a drag race, and yet more than 80 percent of the competitors at na-tional and divisional races operate under a different set of rules. These provide for handicap starts, one driver getting the green sooner than the other, according to an in-tricate and continuously evolving set of indexes relating to elapsed times. The indexes are set by NHRA, but Stock and Super Stock drivers can dial under their indexes if they wish. A car with a dial-in of 15.50, for example, will get a 2.50-second head start over a car with a dial-in of 13.00. A driver who

"breaks out"—runs quicker than the dial-in—will have to confront a tougher handicap.

In the ET brackets, fans see classic street rods and muscle cars, foreign marques, current models, and cars far older than the men and women driving them. Here, under the banner of the Series, drivers compete at the grassroots level that has been the heart and soul of drag racing for more than half a century.

PAT AUSTIN

Pat Austin has run up a total of seventy-one NHRA wins since he started racing in 1986, including five in Top Fuel. A versatile driver, Pat races both Top Fuel dragsters and alcohol Funny Cars and he and his team, Walt Austin Racing, have the distinction of being the only team to win two different Eliminator classes at the same event twice. They won Top Fuel and Top Alcohol Funny Car at both the Heartland Nationals in 1991 and the Motorcraft-Ford Nationals in 1992.

Perhaps these feats should not have come as a surprise, since Pat was named *Car Craft* magazine's All-Star Alcohol Funny Car Driver of the Year for five straight years, from 1987 to 1991. He set speed and ET records in Federal-Mogul Funny Car, and on May 9, 1999, he set a new national record for Top Alcohol Funny Cars with a speed of 253.23 mph and an ET of 5.59. That car exploded two runs later, but Pat came back with a new car and the same resolve, making him a threat in two classes on any given Sunday.

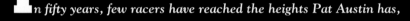

In fifty years, few racers have reached the heights Pat Austin has, with more than seventy wins in an alcohol Funny Car and five during a successful foray in Top Fuel in the mid-1990s.

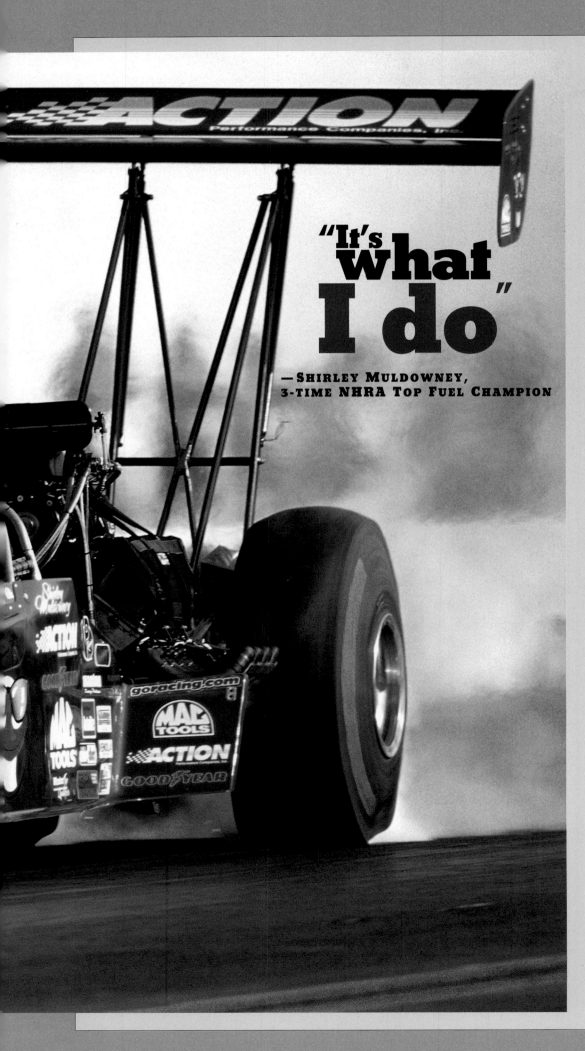

"It's what I do"

— Shirley Muldowney,
3-time NHRA Top Fuel Champion

At national events youngsters are always fighting their way into the top ranks. But what is also striking is the persistence of the veterans, men and women who have been drag racing for thirty, forty, even fifty years, or ever since they were children. By the time the chase for the championship ends on the Pomona Fairgrounds in mid-autumn, the cupboard may be almost bare of spare parts, chassis are dinged, body panels rumpled, and drivers, crew chiefs, and team members are worn out. After every season, a few of the pros throw in the towel, exhausted or broke or both. But, as Wally Parks once remarked, it's always astonishing that so many come back to the tour, rejuvenated and ready to try again, just a few months later.

Once racers have been at the vortex of something so emotionally demanding and yet so rewarding, it becomes hard for them to envision themselves retreating to a world of ordinary routine. Shirley Muldowney, who returned once again to NHRA racing at Indianapolis in 2000, left, said it all years ago when she returned the first time in a new Top Fueler after suffering serious injuries in an accident: "It's what I do." The fans come back as well: It's what they do, and the spectacle never gets old.

Index

Acknowledgments and Photo Credits

The publisher would like to thank the following people and institutions for their help and advice: Wally Parks, Dick Wells, Paula Trujillo, Teresa Long, Marc Gewertz, Ron Lewis, Jerry Foss, Phil Burgess, Rick Voegelin, Dace Taube and the University of Southern California Library, Brad Gerber and the *Hot Rod* Magazine Archives, R. L. "Pete" Garramone, *Post Scripts*, Adriane Pierson, Gary Darcy, Mike Shaffer, Kevin McKenna, John Jodauga, Bruce Dillashaw, and David Kimble.

The publisher would also like to thank the following for their kind permission to reproduce the photographs and illustrations:

Pete Garramone: 66.

Courtesy of University of Southern California on behalf of the Department of Special Collections: 15, 46.

Hot Rod Magazine Archives: 49, 53, 64, 65.

David Kimble: 114–115, 136.

Ron Lewis Photos: 6–7, 8–9, 10–11, 21(T), 32(B), 34, 36–37, 36, 39, 41, 42–43, 43, 44–45, 47, 48, 50–51, 56–57, 57, 60, 61, 62–63, 68, 69, 70, 70–71, 72(B), 75(B), 77, 79, 82, 83, 84–85, 91, 98–99, 101, 102–103, 103, 107, 109, 112, 112–113, 118–119, 119, 120–121, 122(T), 122–123, 124–125, 124, 126–127, 128, 130, 133, 137, 138–1139, 140(L), 141, 142–143, 146, 148, 149(T), 150, 153, 157(T), 160, 161, 162, 165, 167–168, 168, 170, 174–175, 176–177, 180, 181, 183(B), 194–195, 198, 199(T).

NHRA Archives: 1, 2–3, 14, 18, 19, 24–25, 25(T), 27(L), 28(T), 29(B), 31(B), 50, 52, 54(T), 65(R), 66(B), 67, 68(B), 72–73(T), 73(B), 74, 76–77, 86(T), 101, 106, 109, 111(T), 116, 122–123(B), 124(B), 131(B), 134(T), 143, 147(Top four), 152, 153, 157, 184, 193–194, 197(T).

Richard Brady/NHRA: 172–173.

Bill Crites/NHRA: 33, 179(L).

Jerry Foss/NHRA: 20, 34–35, 69(R), 87, 135, 144, 144–145, 156, 160–161, 178(L), 179(R), 186–187.

Marc Gewertz/NHRA: 29(T), 30–31, 32(T), 40, 69(T), 80–81, 86(B), 92(B), 94–95, 104–105, 131,(T), 132(T), 143(T), 149(B), 157(B), 158, 164, 168, 171, 175(T), 176(L), 178(T), 185(T), 188(B), 188–189, 192–193, 200–201.

Teresa Long/NHRA: 4–5, 21(B), 25(R), 27(R), 28(B), 61(B), 90, 136(T), 154, 196–197, 197(R).

Leslie Lovett/NHRA: 38, 69(B), 71(T), 92–93(T), 96–97, 100–101, 106, 110, 111(T), 113(T), 132(T), 138(L), 140(L), 155, 159, 182, 183(T), 190, 191, 199(B).

Wally Parks Collection: 12–13, 16, 16–17, 19, 23, 58–59, 120, 163.

Post Scripts: 22, 23, 47, 48, 54–55(B), 64–65, 75(T), 78, 108, 127.

George Tiedemann: 150.